Also by Mark Myers

A Smarter Way to Learn HTML & CSS

Learn it faster. Remember it longer.

Mark Myers

MARK MYERS

CONTENTS

LEARN IT FASTER.
REMEMBER IT LONGER.

If you embrace this method of learning, you'll get the hang of HTML and CSS in less time than you might expect. And the knowledge will stick.

You'll catch onto concepts quickly.

You'll be less bored, and might even be excited. You'll certainly be motivated.

You'll feel confident instead of frustrated.

You'll remember the lessons long after you close the book.

Is all this too much for a book to promise? Yes, it is. Yet I can make these promises and keep them, because this isn't just a book. It's a book plus 1,800 interactive online exercises. I've done my best to write each chapter so it's easy for anyone to understand, but it's the exercises that are going to turn you into a real HTML coder.

Cognitive research shows that reading alone doesn't buy you much long-term retention. Even if you read a book a second or even a third time, things won't improve much, according to research.

And forget highlighting or underlining. Marking up a book gives us the illusion that we're engaging with the material, but studies show that it's an exercise in self-deception. It doesn't matter how much yellow you paint on the pages, or how many times you review the highlighted material. By the time you get to Chapter 50, you'll have forgotten most of what you highlighted in Chapter 1.

This all changes if you read less and do more—if you read a short passage and then immediately put it into practice. Washington University researchers say that being asked to retrieve information increases long-term retention by four hundred percent. That may seem implausible, but by the time you finish this book, I think you'll believe it.

Practice also makes learning more interesting.

Trying to absorb long passages of technical material puts you to sleep and kills your motivation. Ten minutes of reading followed by twenty minutes of challenging practice keeps you awake and spurs you on.

And it keeps you honest.

If you *only* read, it's easy to kid yourself that you're learning more than you are. But when you're challenged to produce the goods, there's a moment of truth. You *know* that you know—or that you don't. When you find out that you're a little shaky on this point or that, you can review the material, then re-do the exercise. That's all it takes to master this book from beginning to end.

I've talked with many readers who say they thought they had a problem understanding technical concepts. But what looked like a comprehension problem was really a retention problem. If you get to Chapter 50 and everything you studied in Chapter 1 has faded from memory, how can you understand Chapter 50, which depends on your knowing Chapter 1 cold? The read-then-practice approach embeds the concepts of each chapter in your long-term memory, so you're prepared to tackle material in later chapters that builds on top of those concepts. When you're able to remember what you read, you'll find that you learn HTML and CSS quite readily.

I hope you enjoy this learning approach. And then I hope you go on to set the Internet on fire with some terrific webpages.

HOW TO USE THIS BOOK

Since you may not have learned this way before, a brief user manual might be helpful.

- **Study, practice, then rest.** If you're intent on mastering the fundamentals of HTML and CSS, as opposed to just getting a feel for it, work with this book and the online exercises in a 15-to-30-minute session, then take a break. Study a chapter for 5 to 10 minutes. Immediately go to the online links given at the end of each chapter and code for 10 to 20 minutes, practicing the lesson until you've coded everything correctly. Then take a walk.

- **Don't wear yourself out.** You learn best when you're fresh. If you try to cover too much in one day, your learning will go downhill. Most people find they can comfortably cover one to three chapters a day. Your experience may vary.

- **If you find some of the repetition tiresome, skip exercises.** I wrote the exercises for people like me, who need *a lot* of repetition. If you're a fast learner or a learner with some HTML experience, there's no reason to burden yourself. Click the **Skip Exercise and Get Credit** button to jump ahead. Skip whole sets of exercises if you don't need them. Practice as much as you need to, but no more.

- **If you struggle with some exercises, you know you're *really* learning.** An interesting feature of your brain is that the harder it is for you to retrieve a piece of information, the better you remember it next time. So it's actually good news if you have to struggle to recall something from the book. Don't be afraid to repeat a set of exercises. And consider repeating some exercises after letting a few weeks go by. If you do this, you'll be using *spaced repetition*, a power-learning technique that provides even more long-term retention.

- **Do the coding exercises on a physical keyboard.** A

mobile device can be ideal for reading, but it's no way to code. Very, very few Web developers would attempt to do their work on a phone. The same thing goes for *learning* to code. Theoretically, most of the interactive exercises could be done on a mobile device. But the idea seems so perverse that I've disabled online practice on tablets, readers, and phones. (It also simplified my own coding work.)

- **If you have an authority problem, try to get over it.** When you start doing the exercises, you'll find that I can be a pain about insisting that you get every little detail right. For example, if you omit a semicolon, the program monitoring your work will tell you the code isn't correct, even though it might run. Learning to write code with fastidious precision helps you learn to pay close attention to details, a fundamental requirement for coding in any language.

- **Subscribe, temporarily, to my formatting biases.** Current code formatting is like seventeenth-century spelling. Everyone does it his own way. There are no universally accepted standards. But the algorithms that check your work when you do the interactive exercises need standards. They can't grant you the latitude that a human teacher could, because, let's face it, algorithms aren't that bright. So I've had to settle on certain conventions. All of the conventions I teach are embraced by a large segment of the coding community, so you'll be in good company. But that doesn't mean you'll be married to my formatting biases forever. When you begin coding projects, you'll soon develop your own opinions or join an organization that has a stylebook. Until then, I'll ask you to make your code look like my code.

1
HTML & CSS

An HTML (Hypertext Markup Language) document is a text file that tells the browser (Chrome, Firefox, Internet Explorer, Safari, and others) how to assemble a webpage. It says to the browser, "Put this heading here. Put that paragraph there. Insert this picture here. Put that table there."

Though it can create webpages with formatting that is sometimes elaborate and even beautiful, an HTML document itself is pure text, without any formatting whatsoever. This means you can't use a word processing program like Microsoft Word to write HTML, because Word and other word processors add formatting. Instead, you'll choose from any number of editing programs that produce pure text. The simplest of these is Notepad on a PC and TextEdit, in Plain Text mode, on a Mac. You can also use fancier editing programs. And there are web development tools like Dreamweaver. They all create the pure text required for HTML. My favorite code editor is the open source Brackets, free at http://brackets.io/.

When I ask you to do something in Brackets, Notepad, or TextEdit, feel free to substitute any of the alternative editors.

Each HTML document creates a single webpage in the browser. If a site has a hundred pages, it has a hundred HTML documents.

An HTML document's name ends with the **.html** extension, as in **about.html** or **products.html**.

When you're looking at a webpage, you can see the name of the page's HTML document in the browser's address bar.

`http://www.ASmarterWayToLearn.com/htmlcss/23.html`

When the line of characters shown above is entered in the browser's address bar, the browser loads the HTML document **23.html**, and that page is assembled in the browser and displayed on the user's screen. If a user clicks a link on the page for, say **help.html**, then the file **help.html** loads, and that page is displayed.

There's one HTML name you usually won't see in the browser's address bar, `index.html`. That's the name of the page that loads by default when no HTML document is specified. It's the site's *home page*. So if you enter this in the browser's address bar

`http://www.asmarterwaytolearn.com`

…the document that loads (with some exceptions) is `index.html`.

All the HTML documents for a site are stored on the web hosts's server, or, in the case of a big, important site, often on the site owner's own server. When the browser is pointed to a page on the site, the browser fetches the appropriate HTML file from the server and displays that page.

A browser will also display an HTML document stored on your computer's hard drive. That will prompt your browser to display the page on your screen.

Whereas an HTML document specifies the contents of a webpage—the headings, paragraphs, images, tables, etc.—A CSS (*cascading stylesheets*) file specifies the styling of that page—fonts, colors, column widths, and the like.

Like an HTML document, a CSS file is plain text. You can create it with the same editor you use to create an HTML document. A CSS file has the extension `.css`.

When an HTML document loads, it *calls* the CSS file that styles its contents.

Rather than creating a separate CSS file, it's possible to include all of the styling specifications in an HTML document. But the preferred way to style webpages is to put all the styling information in a separate CSS file, so that's what I'm going to teach you.

These are the rules I'm going to ask you to follow for naming both HTML and CSS files:

- Use only lower-case characters.

- Avoid spaces.

- Stick to 0-9, a-z, and _.

Find the interactive coding exercises for this chapter at:
http://www.ASmarterWayToLearn.com/htmlcss/1.html

2
CREATING PARAGRAPHS

Let's get your feet wet.

1. On your hard drive create a folder called **my-smarter-site**. (If you're unclear how to create a folder in your particular operating system, Google it. There's plenty of good Windows and Mac instruction for this online.)

2. Under the **my-smarter-site** folder create a subfolder called **css**. (Again, if this isn't something you know how to do, Google it.)

3. Online, go to http://asmarterwaytolearn.com/htmlcss/practice-2-0.html

4. Copy all the text on the page.

5. Open your plain-text editor (see the last chapter) and create a new document.

6. Paste the copied text into it.

7. Save the document in your **my-smarter-site** folder as **practice.html**

8. On the empty line between **\<body\>** and **\</body\>** type your name.

9. Save the file.

10. Go to Windows Explorer (PC) or Finder (Mac) and double-click the file. And *voila!*

There's your name, displayed in the browser. You've just created and displayed your first webpage.

If it doesn't work, take a look at the sample code at http://asmarterwaytolearn.com/htmlcss/practice-2-1.html

Now, on a new line, add a few more words to your code, so it looks like this.

```
<html>
  <head>
    <title>Practice</title>
  </head>
  <body>
    Mark Myers
    That's my name.
  </body>
</html>
```

Save the file and display the page, following steps 8 and 9 above. (Sample code, if you need it, is at http://asmarterwaytolearn.com/htmlcss/practice-2-2.html.)

But wait! You wrote the text on two lines...

```
    Mark Myers
    That's my name.
```

But the browser displayed it all on one line.

Mark MyersThat's my name.

The problem is that the browser doesn't recognize a carriage return. When you hit a carriage return in a word processor or your text editor, the application breaks the text you write next into a new paragraph, but when you enter a carriage return in an HTML document, the browser ignores it. If you want to display your two sentences in two separate paragraphs, you have to explicitly tell the browser to do it. You do this with paragraph *tags*.

```
<html>
  <head>
    <title>Practice</title>
  </head>
  <body>
    <p>Mark Myers</p>
    <p>That's my name.</p>
  </body>
</html>
```

Revise your practice.html text document to include the tags shown above. Save the file. Display the page in your browser.

If you coded correctly, the page will now display the text in two separate paragraphs.

Sample code is at http://asmarterwaytolearn.com/htmlcss/practice-2-3.html.

Tags are the commonest feature of an HTML document. You use them for all kinds of things. Look at the 9 lines of HTML above. There are tags on every line. Usually—but not always—HTML tags come in pairs, an *opening tag* paired with a *closing tag.* The opening tag consists of some characters enclosed by **<** and **>**. For example, **<p>**. The closing tag is the same as the opening tag, except a **/** follows the opening **<**. For example, **</p>**.

The opening tag tells the browser, "Begin here." The closing tag tells the browser, "End here." So, for example, if you write…

```
<p>These directions are important. Read them carefully.</p>
```

…you're telling the browser to begin the paragraph at "These" and to end it at "carefully."

The browser doesn't care whether you put separate paragraphs on separate lines. As I mentioned above, it ignores carriage returns. But it's conventional to break paragraphs in your code, like this.

```
<p>Hi.</p>
<p>Ho.</p>
```

Things to keep in mind:

- It's legal to write **<P>** instead of **<p>** but I'll ask you to stick to lower-case tags.

- There are no spaces between the tags and the text that they enclose.

- Good housekeeping demands that whenever the browser expects a closing tag, you provide it. Sometimes you can get away with writing **<p>** without closing with **</p>**, but it can produce unpredictable results.

Take good care of the HTML and CSS files you created in this chapter. You'll be revising the files on a regular basis as you make your way through this book. When you complete the book and finish coding the files, you will have *the* worst-looking webpage in Internet history. But it will be a detailed demonstration—a demonstration that *you* made—of the most important concepts in HTML and CSS coding.

Find the interactive coding exercises for this chapter at:
http://www.ASmarterWayToLearn.com/htmlcss/2.html

3
CREATING HEADINGS

A heading on a webpage serves the same purpose as a heading in a newspaper or magazine. It shows the user what's important and gives her a sense of what the paragraphs underneath it are about. Headings also help search engines understand a page.

HTML gives you six sizes of headings to choose from, **h1** through **h6**. **h1** is the largest, **h6** is the smallest.

You don't have to include all the different sizes of headings in your HTML document, but you should include an **h1** heading, because search engines look for it. You can have as many **h2**, **h3**, **h4**, **h5**, and **h6** headings in your document as you want, but you should have only one **h1** heading. Otherwise, search engines might get confused.

This is how you code the largest heading.

```
<h1>This is the largest heading.</h1>
```

Notice that there's both an opening and a closing tag.
Here's a longer one, in **h3** size.

```
<h3>This is a long heading that goes on and on and on, but
it still has just one opening and one closing tag.</h3>
```

Let's look at another heading. If you write…

```
<h3>All the king's horses and all the king's men couldn't
put Humpty together again.</h3>
```

…the browser will break the lines according to how much width is available. It might break the heading like this:

**All the king's horses and all the king's
men couldn't put Humpty together again.**

Or it might break it like this:

> **All the king's horses and all the king's
> men couldn't put Humpty together
> again**

Or maybe it'll break it some other way. But you won't control, and may not be able to predict, how the heading breaks. If you're at all fussy, you might want to tell the browser how to break it. Maybe you want it broken this way:

> **All the king's horses
> and all the king's men
> couldn't put Humpty
> together again.**

So you try writing…

```
<h3>All the king's horses
and all the king's men
couldn't put Humpty
together again.</h3>
```

But this way of writing the heading has no effect on the browser. It still breaks the heading the way *it* wants to. The browser ignores carriage returns.

If you want the browser to break the heading a certain way, you have to tell it to do so explicitly, using the tag **
**.

```
<h3>All the king's horses<br>and all the king's
men<br>couldn't put Humpty<br>together again.</h3>
```

Note that there's no space between the text and **
. And there's no closing **br tag.

By default, browsers separate paragraphs by adding space between them. For example, if you write…

```
<p>Slow lorises are a group of several species of primates
which make up the genus Nycticebus.</p>
<p>They have a round head, narrow snout, large eyes, and
distinctive coloration patterns that are species-
dependent.</p>
```

…the two paragraphs might come out looking something like this:

Slow lorises are a group of several species of strepsirrhine primates which make up the genus Nycticebus.

They have a round head, narrow snout, large eyes, and a variety of distinctive coloration patterns that are species-dependent.

If you wanted a break at the end of the first sentence, but no space between it and the next sentence, you'd consolidate both sentences into a single paragraph and use **
**.

```
<p>Slow lorises are a group of several species of primates
which make up the genus Nycticebus.<br>They have a round
head, narrow snout, large eyes, and distinctive coloration
patterns that are species-dependent.</p>
```

Then it would display like this:

Slow lorises are a group of several species of strepsirrhine primates which make up the genus Nycticebus.
They have a round head, narrow snout, large eyes, and a variety of distinctive coloration patterns that are species-dependent.

The browser displays each heading on its own line. The browser doesn't care whether you put each heading on its own separate line, but for human-readability, please do. For example:

```
<h1>Our Mission</h1>
<h2>Helping People Help People</h2>
```

In your practice.html document replace the two paragraphs about your name with an **h1** heading, an **h2** heading, and a multi-line paragraph. Save the file and display it in your browser. Sample HTML code: http://asmarterwaytolearn.com/htmlcss/practice-3-1.html.

Find the interactive coding exercises for this chapter at:
http://www.ASmarterWayToLearn.com/htmlcss/3.html

4
SPECIFYING FONTS

Browsers display headings and paragraphs in the font of their own choosing. But you can specify the font you want. Let's specify a font for paragraphs.

Open your text editor and create a new file.

1. In the new file type:
```
p {
    font-family: Georgia, "Times New Roman", Times,
    serif;
}
```

2. Save the file as **styles.css** in the **css** subfolder of your **my-smarter-site** folder.

Now you have two files, **practice.html** in the **my-smarter-site** folder and **styles.css** in the **css** subfolder of the **my-smarter-site** folder.

Things to keep in mind:

- There's nothing sacred about calling your HMTL document **practice.html** and your CSS file **styles.css**. You can name the files anything you want, as long as the HTML file has the extension **html** and the CSS file has the extension **css**.

- I've asked you to put the CSS file in a subfolder of your main folder. This is conventional, but not necessary. You could put the CSS file in the same folder as your HTML file if you wanted to, but most developers don't.

Let's look at your CSS code in detail.

It begins with **p**. It means, "This is a style for paragraphs"—that is, all text enclosed by the tags **<p>** and **</p>**.

```
p {
  font-family: Georgia, "Times New Roman", Times, serif;
}
```

p is followed by a space and an opening curly bracket.

```
p {
  font-family: Georgia, "Times New Roman", Times, serif;
}
```

Next, indented 2 spaces, is the specification.

```
p {
  font-family: Georgia, "Times New Roman", Times, serif;
}
```

Notice that it's **font-family**, followed by a colon and a space.

The list of four fonts that follow is known as a *font stack*. If you're specifying a font other than the generic serif, sans-serif, etc., you need to give the browser one or more fallback fonts. (If you're unclear about the difference between serif and sans-serif fonts, Google it.) Fallback fonts are necessary because the browser grabs the fonts for the webpage from the user's computer. If your first font choice isn't installed on the computer, the browser moves on to your second-choice font, then your third-choice font, etc. The stack can list as many fonts as you like, but the common practice is to list three or four. The last fallback—the last font in the stack—is always the generic, for example sans-serif, to guarantee that the browser will be able to display *something* in the family if none of your other choices is found.

If a font name has any spaces in it, enclose it in quotation marks, as in **"Times New Roman"**.

The specification ends with a semicolon.

```
p {
  font-family: Georgia, "Times New Roman", Times, serif;
}
```

Finally, on a line of its own, there's a closing curly bracket.

```
p {
  font-family: Georgia, "Times New Roman", Times, serif;
}
```

Web safe fonts are fonts that have a high likelihood of being found on the user's computer, which makes them good to use on your page. You can find a list of common web safe font stacks at http://abt.cm/O7bwre.

Now let's specify a different font for **h1** headings.

Add this code to your CSS file.

```
h1 {
  font-family: "Trebuchet MS", Helvetica, sans-serif;
}
```

Your CSS file should now include two styles.

```
p {
  font-family: Georgia, "Times New Roman", Times, serif;
}
h1 {
  font-family: "Trebuchet MS", Helvetica, sans-serif;
}
```

Save the file.

Sample CSS code is at http://asmarterwaytolearn.com/htmlcss/practice-4-1.html.

Find the interactive coding exercises for this chapter at:
http://www.ASmarterWayToLearn.com/htmlcss/4.html

5
LINKING YOUR CSS TO YOUR HTML

Since the CSS file is separate from the HTML file, the browser has to be told where to find it. This is how you do it.

```
<html>
  <head>
    <title>Practice</title>
    <link rel="stylesheet" type="text/css"
href="css/styles.css">
  </head>
  <body>
    <p>Mark Myers</p>
    <p>That's my name.</p>
  </body>
</html>
```

This is a mouthful, so let's break it down.

First, notice that the link information goes between the **<head>** and **</head>** tags, rather than between the **<body>** and **</body>** tags, where you wrote your two paragraphs. The difference between the **head** and **body** sections is that the **head** section deals with a few technical matters—like telling the browser where to find the CSS file—while the **body** section contains the content of the page.

Next, notice that the link information itself is a tag. It's placed inside an opening **<** and a closing **>**. But unlike all the other tags you see in the code above, it isn't paired with a closing tag. It stands alone.

The link tag consists of three "equations." Each equation says that something equals something else. The second something is in quotation marks.

1ˢᵗ "equation": **link rel="stylesheet"** tells the browser that the **link rel**ationship is with a **stylesheet**.

2ⁿᵈ "equation": This is a useless, vestigial part of the tag, like your appendix. We've already told the browser the link is to a stylesheet. All stylesheets end with the extension "css," and they're all text documents, so this just repeats what the browser *should* already know. But we still have to include it (but maybe not for long).

3rd "equation": **href** stands for **h**ypertext **ref**erence. This part of the tag tells the browser where to find the CSS file to link to. We've put it in the **css** subfolder of the folder where this HTML document resides, the **my-smarter-site** folder. The file name is "styles.css."

Something to notice about formatting here: There are no spaces in the tag, except those separating the three "equations."

Enter the link tag in your **practice.html** document. Save it, and have your browser display the webpage it creates. Expect the paragraphs to be in a serif font and the heading in a sans-serif font, as you specified in the CSS file.

Find sample HTML code at http://asmarterwaytolearn.com/htmlcss/practice-5-1.html.

Find the interactive coding exercises for this chapter at:
http://www.ASmarterWayToLearn.com/htmlcss/5.html

6
SPECIFYING A FONT-SIZE

Let's change the font-size of your paragraph text and your **h1** heading. Open your **styles.css** file and add the two lines highlighted below.

```
p {
  font-family: Georgia, "Times New Roman", Times, serif;
  font-size: 1.2em;
}
h1 {
  font-family: "Trebuchet MS", Helvetica, sans-serif;
  font-size: 2em;
}
```

When you specify **1.2em** as the paragraph font size, you're saying (without getting too technical) that you want paragraph text to be 1.2 times the default text size—the size that the browser would display if you didn't specify a size. If you specified **1em**, you'd get the default size. **.75em** would be three-quarters of default size. **1.5em** would be 150% of default size. **3.5em** would be three-and-a-half times default size.

This may come as a surprise: When you specify **2em** as the **h1** size, you're not saying you want the **h1** heading to be 200% of the default **h1** size, but 200% of the default *text* size. A **2em** heading is the same size as **2em** paragraph text. The heading, though, will be bold by default and the paragraph won't be.

Things to notice:

- **font-size: 1.2em;** is indented 2 spaces.

- There is no space between **1.2** and **em**.

- The line ends with a semicolon.

Save the CSS file. Display your HTML file.

Find sample CSS code at

http://asmarterwaytolearn.com/htmlcss/practice-6-1.html.

Coding Alternatives to be Aware Of

Instead of specifying font-size in ems, you can specify it in percentages, pixels, or points. In this program we'll stick to ems for font-size.

Find the interactive coding exercises for this chapter at:
http://www.ASmarterWayToLearn.com/htmlcss/6.html

7
CSS CLASSES

You've specified a font family and a font size for paragraphs and **h1** headings. You can also create *classes* of paragraphs and headings with formatting that varies from general styling for paragraphs and headings. In fact, you can create classes of just about any element on the page for custom formatting.

Open your **styles.css** file and add this style...

```
p.important {
  font-size: 1.5em;
}
```

Save your CSS file.

Now you've created special styling for a class of paragraphs. This special style named "important" will override the general style that you created earlier.

When you say you want text in paragraphs of the class "important" to have a font-size of 1.5em, you're saying you want the text to be one-and-a-half times normal size. But what is normal size? It depends on whether you've created a general style in your CSS file that applies to the whole page (See Chapter 19). If you haven't created a general paragraph style, normal size is the browser default size—1em. So then a 1.5em font-size for the paragraph class "important" would be one-and-a-half times the browser default size.

The rules for naming classes would fill a book. To keep things simple, I'm going to ask you to use lowercase alphabet letters, hyphens, underlines, and numbers. But don't start a name with a number. Here's an example of a class for **h3** headings.

```
h3.bigger {
  font-size: 2.5em;
}
```

This class will be 250% of the size of normal text. Again, "normal" means 250% of the size of the browser default text size if you haven't specified a style for the whole page. If you have styled **h3** headings, the "bigger" class of headings will be 250% of *that* size.

Save your CSS file.

Open your HTML file and add this line...

```
<p class="important">Warning: We have no slow lorises
here.</p>
```

Now the text "Warning: We have no slow lorises here." will be one-and-a-half times "normal" text size.

Things to notice:

- The class reference is part of the opening **p** tag, all enclosed in brackets.

- The class name is enclosed in quotation marks.

- The closing paragraph tag doesn't change. It's still **</p>**.

Note: The same class can be assigned to any number of elements. And you can assign more than one class to an element. You just separate the class names by a space. Here's an example.

```
<h3 class="special conspicuous enhanced">Hey now!<h3/>
```

Let's say you've created a class named "special" that specifies a font size, a second class called "conspicuous" that displays it in red, and a third class called "enhanced" that specifies a font-weight of bold. In the example above, all three classes will apply to the heading. It will be extra-large, red, and bold.

Save your files. Display the page. Sample CSS code: http://asmarterwaytolearn.com/htmlcss/practice-7-1.html. Sample HTML code: http://asmarterwaytolearn.com/htmlcss/practice-7-2.html.

Find the interactive coding exercises for this chapter at:
http://www.ASmarterWayToLearn.com/htmlcss/7.html

8
CLASSES NOT TIED TO AN ELEMENT

If you intend to define a particular class for only one type of element—for example, only paragraph text or only **h3** headings—write the element name before the dot and class name, as in…

```
p.special {
```

…or…

```
h3.special {
```

If you want a class to be useable for more than one type of element—for example, both paragraph text and headings—omit the element name. Just write, for example…

```
.special {
```

Open your CSS file and add the style highlighted below.

```
.typewriter {
  font-family: "Courier New", Courier, monospace;
}
```

You've created a new style named "typewriter" that will style text in a typewriter font. It could be paragraph text. It could be heading text. It could be other kinds of text elements that I'll introduce you to later.

Notice that there's no element name, like **p** or **h3**, involved here. It's just a dot with the class name following it.

Save the file.

Open your HTML file and add the section highlighted below.

```
<h2 class="typewriter">This heading is in typewriter text.</h2>
<p class="typewriter">This paragraph is also in typewriter text.</p>
```

You've assigned the class "code" to a heading *and* a paragraph. Since your CSS file doesn't tie the class to any particular element, you can use it for any text element.

Save the HTML file and display it.

Sample CSS code is at
http://asmarterwaytolearn.com/htmlcss/practice-8-1.html. Sample
HTML code is at http://asmarterwaytolearn.com/htmlcss/practice-8-2.html.

Find the interactive coding exercises for this chapter at:
http://www.ASmarterWayToLearn.com/htmlcss/8.html

9
FONT-WEIGHT

In Chapter 7 you created a paragraph class called "important," and specified a font size one-and-a-half times "normal." Now let's make paragraphs classed as "important" even more important. We'll bold them.

Open your CSS file and add the line highlighted below.

```
p.important {
  font-size: 1.5em;
  font-weight: 900;
```

By specifying a font-weight of 900, you're telling the browser to make all the paragraphs of the class **important** as bold as possible. The scale for font-weight ranges from 100 through 900—100, 200, 300 and so on. 100 is the lightest weight. 400 is normal. 900 is as heavy as it gets.

Now, when the browser encounters a paragraph of the **important** class, it will display it larger *and* in boldface.

A note about font-weight: As an alternative to the numerical scale, you can use one of four font-weight words: **lighter**, **normal**, **bold**, and **bolder**.

Save your CSS file. Display your HTML file. "Warning: We have no slow lorises here." should now be in bold.

Find sample CSS code at
http://asmarterwaytolearn.com/htmlcss/practice-9-1.html.

Find the interactive coding exercises for this chapter at:
http://www.ASmarterWayToLearn.com/htmlcss/9.html

10
FONT-STYLE

You can specify italics for any text. Here's a class that applies italics to a paragraph.

```
p.standout {
  font-style: italic;
}
```

Here's a class that applies italics to **h4** headings of the class "special".

```
h4.special {
  font-style: italic;
}
```

Here's a class that applies italics to any text, whether it's a paragraph, heading, or some other text element.

```
.emphasized {
  font-style: italic;
}
```

Remember, class names can be anything you like, within the bounds of the naming rules I covered in Chapter 7.

Instead of defining CSS classes to italicize text, you can use the **<i>** tag in your HTML.

In the following paragraph, the words "David Copperfield" are italicized.

```
<p>Leading style manuals say book titles, like <i>David Copperfield</i>, should be italicized.</p>
```

An alternative to the **<i>** tag is the **<em>** tag.

```
<p>You must be dressed <em>and</em> ready to go.</p>
```

By default, the **<em>** tag has the same visual effect as the **<i>** tag. They both italicize text. The main difference is that when a screen reader sees the **<em>** tag, it puts extra vocal emphasis on the text enclosed in the tag. It doesn't do that with **<i>** text.

41

Instead of creating a class for bold text in CSS, you can use the **<b>** tag in HTML.

In the following paragraph the text "Please note:" is bolded.

```
<p><b>Please note:</b> The flight schedule is subject to change without notice.</p>
```

An alternative to the **<b>** tag is the **<strong>** tag. By default, the **<strong>** tag has the same visual effect as the **<b>** tag. They both bold text in most browsers. The main difference is that when a screen reader sees the **<strong>** tag, the reader may say the text in a lower tone. It doesn't do that with **<b>** text.

In your CSS file, add a class not tied to an element that italicizes text. In your HTML file code a heading of that class. Then write a one-sentence paragraph. In the paragraph, use the two HTML tags that italicize text and the two HTML tags that bold text. Save the files and display your HTML file.

Sample CSS code is at http://asmarterwaytolearn.com/htmlcss/practice-10-1.html. Sample HTML code is at http://asmarterwaytolearn.com/htmlcss/practice-10-2.html.

Find the interactive coding exercises for this chapter at:
http://www.ASmarterWayToLearn.com/htmlcss/10.html

11
STYLING BITS AND PIECES

So far you've been using CSS to style whole blocks of text—paragraphs and headings. But you can also style bits and pieces of those blocks using the **<span>** tag.

Let's go back to the **emphasized** class from the last chapter.

```
.emphasized {
  font-style: italic;
}
```

Since the class, as you defined it, isn't tied to any particular text element—it isn't **p.emphasized** or **h5.emphasized** but just **.emphasized**—it can be applied to any text you choose, including part of a paragraph or heading. In the following paragraph the words "so much" are italicized.

```
<p>I love you <span class="emphasized">so much</span> I
have to use italics.</p>
```

In your HTML file italicize a portion of the paragraph you created in the last chapter, using a span class of "emphasized." Save your HTML file and display it.

Sample HTML code is at
http://asmarterwaytolearn.com/htmlcss/practice-11-1.html.

Find the interactive coding exercises for this chapter at:
http://www.ASmarterWayToLearn.com/htmlcss/11.html

12
COLORS

Let's say you want to display certain text in red. We'll call the class **standout**.

```
.standout {
  color: #cc0000;
}
```

You could, of course, tie the class to a text element. It could be **p.standout** or **h2.standout**, for instance. But we'll make it an all-purpose class so we can use it for any type of text element. Here it is, applied to a single hyphenated word.

```
<p>This is going to be a <span class="standout">red-letter</span> day!</p>
```

Here it is, applied to a whole paragraph.

```
<p class="standout">Please read this chapter carefully.
There <em>will</em> be a quiz.</p>
```

And here it is, applied to a heading.

```
<h1 class="standout">Robots that Care</h1>
```

In the CSS class as I defined it, the color is specified by a hex value, **#cc0000**. You can also use names from the CSS list of colors, like **red**, **gold**, and **mediumslateblue**. Get hex values for colors at http://www.colorpicker.com/. Get a list of CSS color names at http://www.crockford.com/wrrrld/color.html.

In your CSS file create a class not tied to an element that colors text red. In your HTML file use a span to color some text red. Save the files and display your HTML file.

Sample CSS code is at http://asmarterwaytolearn.com/htmlcss/practice-12-1.html. Sample HTML code is at http://asmarterwaytolearn.com/htmlcss/practice-12-2.html.

Find the interactive coding exercises for this chapter at:
http://www.ASmarterWayToLearn.com/htmlcss/12.html

13
SPACING

You can create styles for text spacing. Let's say your **h2** heading normally looks like this.

Sign up for the course now.

If you create this style…

```
h2 {
  letter-spacing: .1em;
}
```

…the **h2** heading would add extra space between the letters. It would look like this…

Sign up for the course now.

Note that when you specify an em value for letter-spacing, it tells the browser how much *more* space you want beyond the normal spacing. Or how much less. Look at this style.

```
h2 {
  letter-spacing: -.05em;
}
```

The code above tightens the space between letters, so the heading looks like this…

Sign up for the course now.

If you wanted to use default letter-spacing, you'd write…

```
h2 {
  letter-spacing: 0;
}
```

Letter-spacing doesn't distinguish between characters in the middle of a word and characters that begin or end a word. This means that letter spacing adjusts the space not only between characters in a word but also between the last character of a word and the first character of the next word. If you increase letter-spacing, the spacing between words increases automatically. If you compare the three examples above, you'll see that space has opened up between words in the first and second examples.

If you want to adjust spacing *only* between words, use **word-spacing**.

I'll exaggerate the word-spacing so you can clearly see it.

```
h2 {
  word-spacing: 1em;
}
```

The CSS above styles the heading to look like this.

Sign   up   for   the   course   now.

You probably won't use word-spacing very often. The most common use for it is to slightly open up the space between bolded words, for better readability.

You can specify the spacing between text lines, known in the analog world as "leading," by using **line-height**.

Here's a paragraph with normal line-height.

Slow lorises are a group of several species of strepsirrhine primates which make up the genus Nycticebus. They have a round head, narrow snout, large eyes, and a variety of distinctive coloration patterns that are species-dependent.

Suppose you create this style.

```
p.more-readable {
  line-height: 2em;
}
```

Any paragraph in the HTML file assigned the class "more-readable" would look like this.

Slow lorises are a group of several species of strepsirrhine primates which make up

the genus Nycticebus. They have a round head, narrow snout, large eyes, and a

variety of distinctive coloration patterns that are species-dependent.

In the case of **line-height**, **1.2em** means normal line spacing. **1.8em** would be roughly an extra half-line of spacing. **1em** would be slightly tighter spacing than normal.

In your CSS file code a paragraph class that increases letter-spacing, word-spacing, and line-height. In your HTML file code a paragraph and assign it that class. Save the files and display your HTML file.

Sample CSS code is at http://asmarterwaytolearn.com/htmlcss/practice-13-1.html. Sample HTML code is at http://asmarterwaytolearn.com/htmlcss/practice-13-2.html.

Find the interactive coding exercises for this chapter at:
http://www.ASmarterWayToLearn.com/htmlcss/13.html

14
ALIGNING TEXT

You can center, left-align, right-align, and justify text. This code centers **h1** headings…

```
h1 {
  text-align: center;
}
```

An **h1** heading that would normally look like this…

Hydrogen Skateboards

…now looks like this…

Hydrogen Skateboards

Left-aligned is the default style for HTML text. But you can make it explicit:

```
p {
  text-align: left;
}
```

Suppose you want to place a date all the way over to the right. You could write…

```
.date-style {
  text-align: right;
}
```

Text assigned that class would look this this. (Look for the date way over on the right.)

July 1, 2018

Here's a paragraph in the default left-aligned style.

Slow lorises are a group of several species of strepsirrhine primates which make up the genus Nycticebus. They have a round head, narrow snout, large eyes, and a variety of distinctive coloration patterns that are species-dependent. Found in Southeast Asia and bordering areas, they range from Bangladesh and Northeast India in the west to the Phillipines in the east, and from Yunnan province in China in the north to the island of Java in the south.

Notice that the right side is "ragged."
If you want to even it up, you could create a style…

```
p.pretty {
   text-align: justify;
}
```

A paragraph assigned the **pretty** class would have an even right edge, like this.

Slow lorises are a group of several species of strepsirrhine primates which make up the genus Nycticebus. They have a round head, narrow snout, large eyes, and a variety of distinctive coloration patterns that are species-dependent. Found in Southeast Asia and bordering areas, they range from Bangladesh and Northeast India in the west to the Phillipines in the east, and from Yunnan province in China in the north to the island of Java in the south.

In your CSS file code all **h3** headings so they center. Create a class of paragraphs that justifies the paragraph. In your HTML file code a centered heading and a justified paragraph.
Sample CSS code is at http://asmarterwaytolearn.com/htmlcss/practice-14-1.html. Sample HTML code is at http://asmarterwaytolearn.com/htmlcss/practice-14-2.html.

Find the interactive coding exercises for this chapter at:
http://www.ASmarterWayToLearn.com/htmlcss/14.html

15
FIRST-LINE INDENT AND BLOCKQUOTE

By default, browsers don't indent the first line of a paragraph. The following paragraph shows how the browser displays a paragraph if you don't tell it to display it differently.

Slow lorises are a group of several species of strepsirrhine primates which make up the genus Nycticebus. They have a round head, narrow snout, large eyes, and a variety of distinctive coloration patterns that are species-dependent.

But you can specify a first-line indent.

```
p {
    text-indent: 1em;
}
```

So now a paragraph would have a first-line indent, like this.

    Slow lorises are a group of several species of strepsirrhine primates which make up the genus Nycticebus. They have a round head, narrow snout, large eyes, and a variety of distinctive coloration patterns that are species-dependent.

Note that any positive **em** value gives you an indent. The larger the value, the deeper the indent.

To explicitly specify the default, no first-line indent, you could write...

```
p {
    text-indent: 0;
}
```

You use **blockquote** to visually set off a quotation that's more than a few words long. By default, any paragraph placed inside **blockquote** tags is indented, like this.

> We hold these truths to be self-evident, that all men are created equal, that they are endowed by their Creator with certain unalienable Rights, that among these are Life, Liberty and the pursuit of Happiness.

This is the HTML.

```
<blockquote><p>We hold these truths to be self-evident,
that all men are created equal, that they are endowed by
their Creator with certain unalienable Rights, that among
these are Life, Liberty and the pursuit of
Happiness.</p><blockquote>
```

You can enclose more than one paragraph in **blockquote** tags. You can enclose headings, too. And if you don't like the default **blockquote** styling, you can change it in your CSS. For example, this code increases the size of the text and displays the text in gray.

```
blockquote {
  font-size: 1.4em;
  color: darkslategray;
}
```

You can even increase or eliminate the amount of blockquote indent. That's in the next chapter.

In your CSS file code a class of paragraphs that indents the first line. Then code a blockquote that decreases the text size and colors the text gray. In your HTML file code a paragraph that indents the first line. Then code a paragraph inside blockquote tags.

Sample CSS code is at http://asmarterwaytolearn.com/htmlcss/practice-15-1.html. Sample HTML code is at http://asmarterwaytolearn.com/htmlcss/practice-15-2.html.

Find the interactive coding exercises for this chapter at:
http://www.ASmarterWayToLearn.com/htmlcss/15.html

16
MARGINS

You can put margins around paragraphs, headings, and many other HTML elements. A margin creates extra whitespace around the top, bottom, or sides of an element. For example, if you have a paragraph that would normally look like this...

Slow lorises are a group of several species of strepsirrhine primates which make up the genus Nycticebus. They have a round head, narrow snout, large eyes, and a variety of distinctive coloration patterns that are species-dependent.

...adding a left margin would add whitespace on the left, like this...

Slow lorises are a group of several species of strepsirrhine primates which make up the genus Nycticebus. They have a round head, narrow snout, large eyes, and a variety of distinctive coloration patterns that are species-dependent.

And adding a right margin, in addition to a left margin, would add whitespace on the right, like this...

Slow lorises are a group of several species of strepsirrhine primates which make up the genus Nycticebus. They have a round head, narrow snout, large eyes, and a variety of distinctive coloration patterns that are species-dependent.

If you wanted, you could specify top and/or bottom margins to add whitespace above and/or below the paragraph. I'll make all the margins extra big so they're easy for you to see. The paragraph would look like this...

> Slow lorises are a group of several species of strepsirrhine primates which make up the genus Nycticebus. They have a round head, narrow snout, large eyes, and a variety of distinctive coloration patterns that are species-dependent

Here's some CSS code that creates a class of paragraphs that I've named **offset** that adds margin space all around the text. The amount of whitespace is two times the size of default text.

```
p.offset {
  margin: 2em 2em 2em 2em;
}
```

A more concise way to code equal margins on all four sides…

```
p.offset {
  margin: 2em;
}
```

When you're specifying all four margins in one statement, you specify them in clockwise order, starting at the top. Let's say you want a right margin twice the size of default text, a left margin 1.75 the size of the font, and no margins on the top or bottom. You'd write…

```
p.offset {
  margin: 0 2em 0 1.75em;
}
```

Note that when you want no margin, you write **0**, not **0em**.

If you want to add space between paragraphs, instead of or in addition to a first-line indent, specify a bottom margin. This code adds space between paragraphs.

```
p {
  margin: 0 0 1em 0;
}
```

Instead of specifying all four margins, you can specify individual margins. An alternative to the example above is…

```
p {
  margin-bottom: 1em;
}
```

You can also specify **margin-top**, **margin-right**, and **margin-left**.

Add a class of paragraphs to your CSS file that has extra whitespace all around it. Then add a paragraph to your HTML document that's in this class. Display the page.

Sample CSS code is at http://asmarterwaytolearn.com/htmlcss/practice-16-1.html. Sample HTML code is at http://asmarterwaytolearn.com/htmlcss/practice-16-2.html.

Find the interactive coding exercises for this chapter at:
http://www.ASmarterWayToLearn.com/htmlcss/16.html

17
BORDERS

You can put a border around a paragraph, a heading, and many other HTML elements that I'll introduce you to in later chapters. The following code demonstrates the simplest way to specify a border. (I made up the class name. You could make up a different name.)

```
p.boxed {
  border: 5px solid red;
}
```

Now any paragraph with the class **boxed** assigned to it will have a 5-pixel-wide, solid, red border on all four sides.

As usual, you don't have to tie the style to a particular element, like a paragraph or heading. You can write, for instance…

```
.enclosed {
  border: 1px dotted #0000ff;
}
```

Now *any* element with the class "enclosed" assigned to it—paragraph, heading, or something else—will have a 1-pixel-wide, dotted, blue border on all four sides.

You can choose among 8 border styles:

- dotted
- dashed
- solid
- double
- groove
- ridge
- inset
- outset

Things to keep in mind:

- There's no space between the number and **px**. It's **2px**, not **2 px**.

- You can use hex values like **#ff00ff** or color names like **blue** to specify colors. Get hex values for colors at http://www.colorpicker.com/. Get a list of CSS color names at http://www.crockford.com/wrrrld/color.html.

- Always state the specs in this order: width, style, color. There's a space between them, but no comma.

You aren't limited just to 4-sided borders. You can specify which sides you want, and can even mix widths, styles, and colors on different sides of the same border (though this wouldn't necessarily be considered good graphic design). Here are some examples.

```
border-top: 4px double red;
border-right: 2px solid #666666;
border-bottom: 6px dashed darkviolet;
border-left: 1px dotted #00ee44;
```

In your CSS file add a class not tied to an element that specifies a border. In your HTML file write a heading of that class. Save the files and display the page.

Sample CSS code is at http://asmarterwaytolearn.com/htmlcss/practice-17-1.html. Sample HTML code is at http://asmarterwaytolearn.com/htmlcss/practice-17-2.html.

Find the interactive coding exercises for this chapter at:
http://www.ASmarterWayToLearn.com/htmlcss/17.html

18
PADDING

When you put a border around a paragraph, heading, or other element, you'll often want to add breathing room—whitespace—between the border and what's inside it. To add a few pixels of whitespace all around, for example, you could write…

```
p.boxed {
  border: 5px solid red;
  padding: .1em;
}
```

The higher the **em** value, the wider the gap between the border and its content.

To specify gaps of different widths for different sides:

```
p.boxed {
  border: 5px solid red;
  padding: .1em .2em 0 .3em;
}
```

The code above specifies a small gap at the top, a larger gap on the right, no gap at the bottom, and the largest gap on the left.

Like code for margins, the numbers start at the top and go clockwise.

You can also specify padding for individual sides. The following code duplicates the effect of the more concise code above.

```
p.boxed {
  border: 5px solid red;
  padding-top: .1em;
  padding-right: .2em;
  padding-bottom: 0;
  padding-left: .3em;
}
```

If you're going to specify padding for all four sides, the more concise code is preferable. But if you want to specify padding for just one or two sides, you might prefer the individual specifications.

Revise your CSS file to include some padding in the class that

specifies a border. Save the file. Display your HTML file.
Sample CSS code is at
http://asmarterwaytolearn.com/htmlcss/practice-18-1.html.

Find the interactive coding exercises for this chapter at:
http://www.ASmarterWayToLearn.com/htmlcss/18.html

19
INHERITANCE

Inheritance is an efficiency feature of CSS. It means you have to write far less code.

In order to understand inheritance, you need to understand that an HTML page is organized into *parents* and *children*. A child element of a parent element is any element that's enclosed by the parent element.

Let's start with the *uber*-parent. In an HTML document, the parent of all the content that displays on the page is **<body>**. Everything on the page is a child of **<body>**, because every element is enclosed by the **<body>** tags. (Both **<head>** and **<body>** have a parent, **<html>**, but we're not concerned with that now.)

Look at the simplified webpage from Chapter 2.

```
<html>
  <head>
    <title>Practice</title>
  </head>
  <body>
    <p>Mark Myers</p>
    <p>That's my name.</p>
  </body>
</html>
```

The two paragraphs, like everything else we might add to the page, are enclosed by the opening and closing **<body>** tags, so they are all children of **<body>**. As the body element's children, they inherit all the CSS properties of that element. So, for example, if we style the body element like this…

```
body {
  font-family: Georgia, "Times New Roman", Times, serif;
  font-size: 1.2em;
  color: darkslategray;
}
```

…all the text on the page will display in Georgia or one of the alternatives, at 1.2 times the default size, and in gray. Paragraphs will be in Georgia or one of its alternatives. So will headings. All text will be based on a "normal" text size of 1.2 times the browser's default text size. All text, whether paragraphs or headings, will be gray. Unless…

…you override the inheritance.

For example, if you include this style in your CSS…

```
h2 {
   font-family: "Trebuchet MS", Helvetica, sans-serif;
}
```

…it overrides the inherited font-family, Georgia or its relatives, and styles all **h2** headings in Trebuchet or its relatives. Since you haven't specified any overriding styles for size or color, the **h2** headings will inherit these styles as specified for the parent, the body element. **h2** headings will be 120% the size of the default for **h2** headings, and they'll be gray. Of course, you can override these inherited styles as well, for example:

```
h2 {
   font-family: "Trebuchet MS", Helvetica, sans-serif;
   font-size: .5em;
   color: black;
}
```

Now we've overridden all the inherited styles.

When you override an inherited size with an **em** value as in the code above, the new **em** value is *relative to the inherited size*. The style that the **h2** heading in the code above inherits from the body element is **1.2em**— 1.2 times the default text size. So when we style the **h2** heading at **.5em**, we're saying, "Make **h2** headings half the inherited size." The inherited size, thanks to the style of the body element, is 1.2 times the default size. Half of that size, specified by **.5em**, is .6 times the default size.

That's pretty confusing, which is why many developers specify **1em** for font-size in the body style. That makes it clear that all **em** values specified for other elements will be relative to the browser's default size.

Find the interactive coding exercises for this chapter at:
http://www.ASmarterWayToLearn.com/htmlcss/19.html

20
GROUPING

You can group elements that share one or more style characteristics. For example, if **h1**, **h3**, and **h5** headings are all to be in the Arial font or one of its relatives and you want them all centered, you can write...

```
h1, h3, h5 {
  font-family: Arial, Helvetica, sans-serif;
  text-align: center;
}
```

Now all three types of headings share the same font-family and text alignment.

This doesn't prevent you from individually styling these elements with other characteristics. For example, if you want **h1** and **h5** headings in one color and **h3** headings in another color, you could add this code...

```
h1, h5 {
  color: #333333;
}
h3 {
  color: #999999;
}
```

Now all three heading types share the same font-family and text alignment. **h1** and **h5** headings are one color. And **h3** headings are another color.

In your CSS file group **h4** headings and a class of paragraphs that center. In your HTML file code an **h4** heading and a paragraph of that class. Save the files and display the page.

Sample CSS code is at http://asmarterwaytolearn.com/htmlcss/practice-20-1.html. Sample HTML code is at http://asmarterwaytolearn.com/htmlcss/practice-20-2.html.

Find the interactive coding exercises for this chapter at:
http://www.ASmarterWayToLearn.com/htmlcss/20.html

21
ID

At this point you should be clear about CSS classes. They can be tied to an element, like this.

```
p.extra-special {
  font-style: italic;
}
```

Or they can be for general use—that is, not tied to any particular element, like this.

```
.extra-special {
  font-style: italic;
}
```

In HTML you assign a class to an element like this.

```
<p class="extra-special">Daily Special<p/>
```

A class can be assigned to any number of elements. And an element can be assigned any number of classes. If you have a paragraph class, it can be assigned to a thousand different paragraphs if you like. If you have a class that isn't tied to a particular element, it can be assigned to different kinds of elements.

An *id* is like a class, but more exclusive. It can be assigned only once in an HTML document. And an element, though it can have many classes, can have only one id.

For example, suppose you're styling a paragraph that contains a mission statement. This particular styling won't be used for any other paragraph. You could style this special paragraph with a class, but it would be clearer, from a human point of view, to single it out as unique by assigning it an id.

The following code creates an id and styling for the mission statement.

```
p#mission-statement {
  font-family: "Times New Roman", Times, serif;
  font-size: 1.2em;
  color: darkblue;
}
```

Note that in the CSS the syntax you use to define ids is exactly the same as for classes, except that a **#** replaces the dot.

The following code creates a heading id.

```
h2#product-features {
  font-family: "Trebuchet MS", Helvetica, sans-serif;
  color: blue;
}
```

The following code creates an id that can be used for a paragraph, a heading, or other elements that you'll learn about later. But remember, any id, including this one, should be used only once on any HTML page. For example, if you use it for a paragraph, don't use it for another paragraph, a heading, or any other element on the page.

```
#special {
  font-size: 1.5em;
  font-style: italic;
}
```

Here's an example of HTML that assigns an id to an element.

```
<p id="whatever">This paragraph has a unique id.</p>
```

In the HTML the syntax is exactly the same, except that you replace **class** with **id**.

ids play an even larger role in JavaScript, as you'll learn in my book *A Smarter Way to Learn JavaScript*, available at Amazon.

In your CSS file code an **h2** id that colors the heading orange. In your HTML file code a heading with that id. Save the files. Display the page.

Sample CSS code is at http://asmarterwaytolearn.com/htmlcss/practice-21-1.html. Sample HTML code is at http://asmarterwaytolearn.com/htmlcss/practice-21-2.html. Find the interactive coding exercises for this chapter at: http://www.ASmarterWayToLearn.com/htmlcss/21.html

22
DIV

You can break up a webpage into sections, called *divs*. Each of these **div**s can have its own styling, using either a class or an id. Coders commonly create separate **div**s for headers, navigation bars, main content, and footers. Here's some code that creates a **div** for the main content of the page. Since there would be only one such section, I use an id rather than a class.

```
div#main {
  font-size: 1.1em;
  margin: .1em .2em .2em .2em;
}
```

Here's the HTML that assigns the id.

```
<div id="main">
  <h2>Here's the whole story.</h2>
  <p>It's soft.</p>
  <p>It's fluffy.</p>
</div>
```

All elements within this **div** will be contained in a section that has a margin on each side. Unless you've written overriding CSS code that changes the font-size of certain text elements, all elements in the **div**, which are children of the **div**, will be 110% of "normal" size (however you've defined "normal" when you styled the body). If those individual text elements are styled smaller (less than **1em**) or larger (more than **1em**) than normal, they'll be scaled up or down in relation to the **1.1em** specified for the **div**, not the "normal" specified for the body. So if you specified **1em** (the browser's default size) for the body, **1.1em** for the **div**, and **1.5em** for **h3** headings, the headings will be 150% of 110% of the browser's default text size.

Note that the **<div>** tag is closed, and that the elements that are enclosed by the **<div>** tags are indented 2 spaces, since they're all children of the **div**.

When you're styling a **div** that appears only once on the page, like

69

the navigation section, main content, or footer, it's best to create an id rather than a class for it. If there's a possibility a **div** style may be used more than once, define a class. For example:

```
div.special {
  margin: .1em .5em .1em .5em;
}
```

Any **div** assigned the "special" class will have extra margins on the left and right. The result is that it will be inset.

Add a **div** id to your CSS file. Give it **3em** left and right margins. Assign it the font family Arial, Helvetica, sans-serif. In your HTML file code a **div** with that id. Inside the **div** code a heading and paragraph. Save the files and display the page.

Sample CSS code is at http://asmarterwaytolearn.com/htmlcss/practice-22-1.html. Sample HTML code is at http://asmarterwaytolearn.com/htmlcss/practice-22-2.html.

Find the interactive coding exercises for this chapter at:
http://www.ASmarterWayToLearn.com/htmlcss/22.html

23
IMAGES

Images on a webpage are almost always one of three types: jpg, gif, or png. In each case, the three initials refer to the file extension that denotes the image format. The jpg format is best for photographs and for illustrations with many subtle colors. The gif format can be used for line drawings, illustrations with just a few colors, and images of text. Gifs offer transparency, meaning that the background color can show through wherever you want it to. Gifs can be animated. Unless you need animation, the gif format is rarely your best choice. The png format is better. It has the same general features as gif, but has no animation. It's preferred over gif because it gives you higher quality than a gif and in a smaller file size. A smaller file size means pages load faster.

An HTML file tells the browser which images to place on the page and where to place them, but the images themselves aren't part of the HTML file. They're individual jpg, gif, or png files that can be stored anywhere on the Internet. In practice, they're usually placed in a subfolder under the site's main folder. The name most often used for the subfolder is "images."

Let's assume that your site's images are in the "images" subfolder of your site's main folder. This is how to place an image called "founder.jpg" on your page.

```
<img src="images/founder.jpg">
```

img src stands for "image source." It tells the browser where to find the image. An equal sign comes next. Then there's the path and file name, all in quotes.

There is no closing tag.

In the normal flow of HTML code, an image will be placed on the page in the same location as it appears in the code. For example, in the following code…

```
<h3>Our founder</h3>
<img src="images/founder.jpg">
<p>Our founder is no longer with us, alas.<p/>
```

…the photo appears under the heading and before the paragraph.

You can, although often not legally, display an image from another website. In that case, you have to include the whole URL.

```
<img src="http://www.asmarterwaytolearn.com/surprise.jpg">
```

The following displays an image stored in the subfolder "pics" of my website.

```
<img
src="http://www.asmarterwaytolearn.com/pics/loris.jpg">
```

Unless you tell it otherwise in your CSS file, the browser will place an image all the way over on the left. Later, you'll learn how to place it where you want it—for example, in the center of the page.

Add an image to your HTML file: http://www.asmarterwaytolearn.com/loris.jpg. Save the file and display it.

Sample HTML code is at http://asmarterwaytolearn.com/htmlcss/practice-23-1.html.

Find the interactive coding exercises for this chapter at: http://www.ASmarterWayToLearn.com/htmlcss/23.html

24
BLOCK VS. INLINE

Most major HTML elements—headings, paragraphs, lists, tables, and **div**s—are *block* elements. When an element is a block element, it means the browser doesn't put any other element beside it. If you write a heading, then a paragraph, then a list, the heading will begin on a new line. The paragraph will begin on a new line. The list will begin on a new line.

Block elements *can* be placed side-by-side, but only if you specify special styling. **Div**s are block elements, but we place them side-by-side all the time using something called **float**, for example when we place a sidebar next to a content section. You'll learn more about this later.

All block elements inside a **div** own their own horizontal space only inside that **div**. If your CSS specifies that two **div**s are to be placed side-by-side, then of course elements of one **div** will sit next to elements of the other **div**. It'll be like two columns, with each element having its own horizontal space, but only within its column.

In addition to starting each block element on a new line, the browser will add extra space between them. Later you'll learn to adjust this space using CSS.

Inline elements don't start on a new line. For example, a link is an inline element. If you write…

```
<p>To find the color that complements your complexion, try
our <a href="color-picker.html">Color Picker</a>.</p>
```

…the **a href** element doesn't start on a new line. That's good, because you want it to be part of the sentence flow, not set off.

You may find it surprising that images are inline rather than block elements. If you write…

```
<img src="pic-1.jpg">
<img src="pic-2.jpg">
<img src="pic-3.jpg">
```

…the three images will be arrayed across the **div**, if there's room for them all.

You can convert images into block elements using CSS.

```
img.owns-its-own-line {
  display: block;
}
```

Now any image assigned to the class "owns-its-own-line" won't share horizontal space with other images.

In your CSS file code a class of images that displays as a block. In your HTML file assign that class to the loris image that you've already coded. Then duplicate that image tag. Now you have two images of the loris. Save the files and display the page.

Sample CSS code is at http://asmarterwaytolearn.com/htmlcss/practice-24-1.html. Sample HTML code is at http://asmarterwaytolearn.com/htmlcss/practice-24-2.html.

Find the interactive coding exercises for this chapter at:
http://www.ASmarterWayToLearn.com/htmlcss/24.html

25
ADDING MORE INFO TO THE IMAGE TAG

In the last chapter you learned to write the minimal amount of code for placing an image on the page.

```
<img src="images/founder.jpg">
```

This tag gives the browser the name of the image file and the path where it's stored. That will get the job done. In practice, though, you'll want to write a more elaborate tag.

```
<img src="images/founder.jpg" alt="Our founder" width="55" height="85">
```

The **alt** specification provides a word or a few words that describe the image. It's the text **alt**ernative to the image, which the browser may display in case the browser fails to display the image for some reason or a person is using a screen reader. The text is up to you, but it should be brief.

The width and height specifications tell the browser how big the image is to be when it's displayed. The numbers are pixels.

The common practice is to size original images to exactly the dimensions that they'll display in the browser. So, in the example above, the image **founder.jpg** would be saved in Photoshop or another image editing program 55 pixels wide and 85 pixels high. Stating the dimensions in the image tag gives the browser a head-start on displaying the image correctly, which speeds up loading.

The dimensions you specify in the image tag don't have to be the same as the dimensions of the image. For example, if you have an image that's 200 pixels wide by 300 pixels high, you could ask the browser to scale it to 50% by writing **width="100" height="150"**. You could also ask the browser to scale up an image, but this is rarely done, since it degrades the image.

Asking the browser to rescale an image slows down page loading minutely. If you have many images on your page, there might be a noticeable delay.

Browsers don't care about the order in which you specify **src**, **alt**, **width**, and **height**, but the order I've given is conventional. I'll ask you to stick to it in the exercises. A reader and beta tester, John Koch, remembers the order of the first three specifications by thinking of a SAW.

In your HTML file add an **alt** specification to both loris image tags. Also add width and height specifications. The image size is 250 x 197. Specify that for the first image. Specify 125 x 99 for the second image. Save the file and display the page.

Sample HTML code is at http://asmarterwaytolearn.com/htmlcss/practice-25-1.html.

Find the interactive coding exercises for this chapter at:
http://www.ASmarterWayToLearn.com/htmlcss/25.html

26
POSITIONING AN IMAGE

If you don't tell the browser where you want an image placed, the browser will place it all the way over on the left. It'll also array consecutive images side-by-side across the screen if there's room.

You can isolate an image on its own line by letting the browser know that you want the image treated as a block, not an inline element. When it's treated as a block, it gets to monopolize the horizontal space it sits in.

As you've learned, this is how you tell the browser to treat an image as a block.

```
img.normal {
  display: block;
}
```

Even though the browser positions an image all the way over on the left by default, you can move it to the right as far as you like, using margins. The following code defines an image class that moves an image slightly to the right of the left edge of the page or of the **div** that contains it.

```
img.inset {
  display: block;
  margin-left: 1em;
}
```

If you wanted it farther to the right, you'd increase the **em** number.

A reminder: **inset** is a name I made up. You can name a class anything you like as long as you follow the naming rules.

In your CSS file create a class that moves an image right. In your HTML file add that class to the second loris image. Remember, an element can have more than one class assigned to it. So the image will have both the class "has-own-line" and the class "inset." Save the files and display the page.

Sample CSS code is at http://asmarterwaytolearn.com/htmlcss/practice-26-1.html. Sample

HTML code is at http://asmarterwaytolearn.com/htmlcss/practice-26-2.html.

Find the interactive coding exercises for this chapter at:
http://www.ASmarterWayToLearn.com/htmlcss/26.html

27
CENTERING AN IMAGE

Let's create a class for centering images. I'm going to give it a ridiculous name, to remind you that class names are made up.

```
img.smack-in-the-middle {
  display: block;
  margin-left: auto;
  margin-right: auto;
}
```

auto tells the browser to split the left and right margins equally. The result is a centered image.

Here's the HTML.

```
<img class="smack-in-the-middle" src="images/founder.jpg"
alt="Our founder" width="55" height="85">
```

Note that in the HTML above **class** comes before **src** and all the other specifications. This isn't strictly necessary, but I'll ask you to follow the convention when you do the exercises.

An alternative way to code the styling:

```
img.smack-in-the-middle {
  display: block;
  margin: 0 auto 0 auto;
}
```

In your CSS file code a class of images that centers. In your HTML file add a third loris image and assign it this class. Save the files and display the page.

Sample CSS code is at http://asmarterwaytolearn.com/htmlcss/practice-27-1.html. Sample HTML code is at http://asmarterwaytolearn.com/htmlcss/practice-27-2.html.

Find the interactive coding exercises for this chapter at:
http://www.ASmarterWayToLearn.com/htmlcss/27.html

28
FLOATING IMAGES

Would you like to wrap some text around an image? Here's how.

```
img.wrap-around-the-right-side {
  float: left;
}
```

Now any text that comes after the image in your HTML code will wrap around the image, on the right. If the text is too long to fit completely next to the image, it'll continue at full width under the image.

Note that there's no **display: block** here. The image will share its horizontal space if there's room.

If you want text to wrap around the left side of the image, you'd write:

```
img.r-float {
  float: right;
}
```

When you do this, you'll notice that the browser jams the text up against the image, leaving no breathing room. You can correct this by adding some margin to the image. In the following code, whitespace is added between the image and the text on its right. Whitespace is also added below the image, to give breathing room between the image and any text that flows beneath the image.

```
img.wrap-around-the-right-side {
  float: left;
  margin: 0 .75em .5em 0;
}
```

There's one unintended consequence you need to avoid. Let's say you have a short paragraph wrapping around the left side of an image. The paragraph is so short that it doesn't fill all the space to the left of the image. If you add another paragraph under the short paragraph, it will wrap. If you don't want this, you need to tell the browser to **clear** the float after the first paragraph. To do this, you create a class.

```
p.no-wrap {
  clear: both;
}
```

By telling the browser to clear **both**, you're saying, "Don't wrap anything from here on." Here's the HTML.

```
<img class="wrap-around-the-right-side"
src="images/founder.jpg" alt="Our founder" width="55"
height="85">
<p>This is our founder, Bradley B. Bradley, who envisioned
a Brad's Breadsticks on every corner.</p>
<p class="no-wrap">Wherever you go, you'll find a Brad's
Breadsticks nearby, with breadsticks in 43 delicious
flavors.</p>
```

1. In your CSS file code a class of images that floats and creates some space between it and the text that wraps around it.

2. Create a class of paragraphs that clears the wrap.

3. In your HTML file copy the image tag for the smaller version of the loris. Replace the class name with the class that floats.

4. Code a paragraph that will wrap around the image.

5. Code a paragraph that clears the wrap.

6. Save the files and display the page.

Sample CSS code is at http://asmarterwaytolearn.com/htmlcss/practice-28-1.html. Sample HTML code is at http://asmarterwaytolearn.com/htmlcss/practice-28-2.html.

Find the interactive coding exercises for this chapter at:
http://www.ASmarterWayToLearn.com/htmlcss/28.html

29
LINKS

Now we come to the feature for which HTML is named, *hypertext* a.k.a. *hyperlinks* a.k.a. *links*. You click on some text or an image, and a new page loads. Or perhaps something else happens.

A link is displayed, by default, in blue, with an underline. Let's say I want to have a link on my site, A Smarter Way to Learn, that takes the user to the programming site Stack Overflow. When the user clicks Stack Overflow, he is taken to the home page of that site. This is the HTML that creates the link:

```
<a href="http://www.stackoverflow.com">Stack Overflow</a>
```

These are the parts.

- **a** tells the browser to watch for an *anchor*. The anchor is the *link text* between the opening **<a>** tag and the closing **</a>** tag. It is the text that the user sees. In this case the anchor, or link text, is Stack Overflow.

- **href** stands for "hypertext reference." **href** tells the browser, "Watch for an address immediately following the equal sign. This will be the page to load when the user clicks the anchor."

- The Web address is in quotes. In this case the address is **http://www.stackoverflow.com**.

- After the opening tag comes the anchor, the text that the user clicks to tell the browser to execute the link. The anchor is *not* in quotes.

- The closing tag ends it.

If you're linking to a page on the same website, in the same folder, all you need is the page name:

```
<a href="products.html">Our products</a>
```

If it's on the same website but in a subdirectory, you add the subdirectory name. In the following code, the file is in the catalog subdirectory.

```
<a href="catalog/products.html">Our products</a>
```

In your HTML file code a link to Stack Overflow at http://www.stackoverflow.com". Save the file and display the page. Click the link.

Sample HTML code is at http://asmarterwaytolearn.com/htmlcss/practice-29-1.html.

Find the interactive coding exercises for this chapter at:
http://www.ASmarterWayToLearn.com/htmlcss/29.html

30
LINK ADDRESSES

When a link address doesn't specify a page, like **about.html**, the browser goes to the home page of the site, usually called **index.html**.

http://www.stackoverflow.com is the same as **http://www.stackoverflow.com/index.html**

If I wanted to link to a page *other than* **index.html**, I would include the page name in the address, like...

http://www.stackoverflow.com/web-design.html

Note that there's a **/** between the domain name and the page name. There are no spaces.

If the page I wanted to link to were in a subfolder under the main folder, I'd include the subfolder name as well:

http://www.stackoverflow.com/questions/web-design.html

A link might drill down through additional levels of subdirectories, to get to a page. For example:

http://www.stackoverflow.com/questions/rookie/newest/web-design.html

You don't have to have several levels of subdirectories in your site structure, but you might want to for purposes of organization if the site has hundreds of pages. If it's a simple site, you might have, for example, just an "images" subfolder and a "styles" subfolder under the main folder. All the HTML pages would be in the main folder. Or you might choose a flat structure, with no subdirectories at all. It's up to you.

When you link to a page on your own site, you can skip the domain name. For example, if I want to display a link on the home page of my site that takes the user to my own site's **faq** page, I won't have to write...

```
<a href="http://www.asmarterwaytolearn.com/faq.html">Frequently Asked Questions</a>
```

I can write, simply...

```
<a href="faq.html">Frequently Asked Questions</a>
```

When I omit the domain name, the browser understands that I'm linking to a page on the same site.

If the page I'm linking to is on the same site but in a folder or several levels of directories lower than the folder you're linking from, you can still skip the domain name, but you have to include the name(s) of the lower folder or directories.

```
<a href="services/code-checking.html">Frequently Asked
Questions</a>
```

In the example above, you're telling the browser that the page **code-checking.html** is one level below the folder you're linking from, in the subfolder **services**. Note that there is no **/** before the subfolder name.

But suppose you want to link from a page in the **services** subfolder to a page in the **products** subfolder that's on the same level as the **services** subfolder. So now you have to tell the browser to first go back up one level, and then go down from there to the **products** subfolder. This is how you do it.

```
<a href="../products/text-editors.html">Frequently Asked
Questions</a>
```

For each level the browser needs to go back up in order to go down again, add an additional **../**

For example, suppose you're writing a link on a page that's in a folder two levels down from the home page. To link back to the home page (**index.html**), you'd write:

```
<a href="../../index.html">Home</a>
```

In your HTML file create a brief paragraph that includes a link that takes the user to the why-exercises.html page at smarterwaytolearn.com. Save the file and display the page. Click the link.

Sample HTML code is at http://asmarterwaytolearn.com/htmlcss/practice-30-1.html. Find the interactive coding exercises for this chapter at:
http://www.ASmarterWayToLearn.com/htmlcss/30.html

31
LINKING TO A LOCATION ON A PAGE

When you create a page of significant length, you might want to provide links to various sections of the page, so the user doesn't have to scroll through the page looking for the section she wants to see. On a long page, it's also nice to provide links to the top of the page, so when she's finished with a lower section, she can jump back to the top.

You begin by choosing a heading, paragraph, or other element to serve as the starting point for the section. You give this element an id.

```
<h2 id="fame-claim">OUR CLAIM TO FAME</h2>
```

Then you create a link to it.

```
<a href="#fame-claim">Read all about our claim to fame.</a>
```

It's like links you learned about in the last chapter, except that a **#** precedes the id in the reference.

To insert a link back to the top, you'd create an id for an element at or near the top of the page. It could be the main heading for the page. Or it could be the **content div** that encompasses all the content on the page.

```
<div class="content" id="top">
```

Then, wherever you want to place the link, you could write…

```
<a href="#top">Back to the top</a>
```

When you want to link to a location on another page on the same site, you have to include the name of the page.

```
<a href="faq.html#why-me">Get answers to your cosmic
questions</a>
```

The code above links to a heading, paragraph, or other element with the id **why-me** on the **faq.html** page.

When you want to link to a section of a page on another site, you have to include the domain name.

```
<a href="http://www.cosmicquestions.com/faq.html#why-
me">Get answers to your cosmic questions</a>
```

In order for this to work, the page on the other site has to have an element with the id "why-me."

In your HTML file give the heading at the top of the page an id. At the bottom of the page code a link to that heading. Save the file and display the page. Scroll down to the link and click it.

Sample HTML code is at http://asmarterwaytolearn.com/htmlcss/practice-31-1.html.

Find the interactive coding exercises for this chapter at:
http://www.ASmarterWayToLearn.com/htmlcss/31.html

32
OPENING A NEW WINDOW

No one ever wants to lose a user to another site, but sometimes we have to link away anyway. The tactic for encouraging the user not to leave permanently is to open the linked site in a new window, leaving your site in its existing window. This is how to do it.

```
Look it up at <a href="http://www.wikipedia.org"
target="_blank">Wikipedia</a>.
```

When the user clicks the link text **Wikipedia** a new window opens for Wikipedia. The original page remains open in its own window.

Have you seen link text that says things like "Explain this" or "What is this"? When you click one of these links, a small window opens on top of the main window with a bit of useful information. Most of the main window still shows, so the user doesn't get disoriented. She sees the little window as an addendum to the main window. Unfortunately, you can't create one of these little informational windows in HTML. You need JavaScript. My book *A Smarter Way to Learn JavaScript* shows you how, step-by-step. But here's some code that you can paste into your page if you'd like to create a small window without knowing JavaScript.

```
<p id="openWindow">Tell me a little more about this.</p>
<script>
document.getElementById("openWindow").onclick = openWindow;
function openWindow() {
  var w = window.open("more-info.html", "",
"width=200,height=300,left=300,top=400");
}
</script>
```

Adapt the script above to your needs by making these changes:

- Substitute your anchor for **Tell me a little more about this.**

- Substitute your HTML file name for **more-info.html**

- Substitute your preferred width and height for **width=200,height=300**. The numbers are pixels.

- Substitute your preferred window placement on the screen for **left=300,top=400**. The first number tells the browser how many pixels to inset the window from the left edge of the screen. The second number tells the browser how many pixels to drop the window from the top of the screen.

Don't add or delete any spaces from the code. The spacing may look odd, but if you try to improve it in any of the wrong places, the window won't open.

In your HTML file code a paragraph that includes a link to asmarterwaytolearn.com. Save the file and display it. Click the link.

Sample HTML code is at http://asmarterwaytolearn.com/htmlcss/practice-32-1.html.

Find the interactive coding exercises for this chapter at:
http://www.ASmarterWayToLearn.com/htmlcss/32.html

33
STYLING LINKS

By default browsers style link text in blue with an underline. But you can give it a different style. You can specify a different font-family, font-size, font-weight, color, and other font characteristics.

You can even lose the underline if you like. But be careful. Users have been conditioned to associate the underline with links. If there's no underline, they'll have a harder time identifying text as something they can click. Conversely, it's a bad idea to underline non-linking text for emphasis. Some users will try to click on it. For emphasis, it's better to put non-linking text in italics or bold.

This CSS code colors all your links goldenrod.

```
a {
  color: #b8860b;
}
```

You can make links change their appearance when the user hovers the mouse over them. This code bolds them and removes the underline when the user hovers. (Removing the underline on hover isn't a problem, because the user has already identified it as a link.)

```
a:hover {
  font-weight: bold;
  text-decoration: none;
}
```

In the code above, **text-decoration: none** removes the underline.

It's not a good idea to underline nonlinking text since it may confuse the reader by signalling that the text is clickable, but you *can* underline text if you choose to, by specifying **text-decoration: underline**.

You can change the appearance of links at the moment the user clicks. This code increases their size on the click.

```
a:active {
    font-size: 1.25em;
}
```

You can change the appearance of links that the user has already clicked. This code changes their color.

```
a:visited {
    color: deeppink;
}
```

In your CSS file code links grey and links that are hovered on orange. Save the file. Display the page. Check the links. Hover over one and see what happens.

Sample CSS code is at
http://asmarterwaytolearn.com/htmlcss/practice-33-1.html.

Find the interactive coding exercises for this chapter at:
http://www.ASmarterWayToLearn.com/htmlcss/33.html

34
CLICKABLE IMAGES

You can substitute an image for a link anchor (the text that the user clicks). When the user clicks on the image, it works the same as anchor text: a new page loads or something else happens. To do it, you combine two tags you already know, the **a** tag and the **img** tag.

Look again at the link code from Chapter 28.

```
<a href="http://www.stackoverflow.com">Stack Overflow</a>
```

When the user clicks the words "Stack Overflow" she's taken to stackoverflow.com.

Here's some code that uses the Stack Overflow logo instead of an anchor.

```
<a href="http://www.stackoverflow.com"><img
src="images/stack-overflow-logo.png alt="Stack Overflow
logo" width="85" height="25"></a>
```

When the user clicks the image, she's taken to stackoverflow.com

One way to create a clickable button is to make an image of a button, then make the image clickable.

```
<a href="faq.html"><img src="images/button-faq.png
alt="Button linking to FAQ page" width="50"
height="18"></a>
```

Another good use for clickable images is a photo gallery. You array one or more rows of thumbnail images across the page. When the user clicks one of them, a larger version of the image loads in a new window. Here's code that turns an array of thumbnails into a clickable catalog.

```
<a href="full-size-robin.html"><img class="fl-left"
src="images/thumbnail-1.jpg" alt="Robin" width="50"
height="50"></a>
<a href="full-size-blue-jay.html"><img class="fl-left"
src="images/thumbnail-2.jpg" alt="Blue Jay" width="50"
height="50"></a>
<a href="full-size-cardinal.html"><img class="fl-left"
src="images/thumbnail-3.jpg" alt="Cardinal" width="50"
height="50"></a>
<a href="full-size-sparrow.html"><img class="fl-left"
src="images/thumbnail-4.jpg" alt="Sparrow" width="50"
height="50"></a>
<a href="full-size-pigeon.html"><img class="fl-left"
src="images/thumbnail-5.jpg" alt="Pigeon" width="50"
height="50"></a>
```

A nice way to do this is to add **target="_blank"** to the **a** tag as I showed you in Chapter 32, so the page with the big picture opens in a new window. Even nicer: open it in a window that's smaller than full-size so the user can see a portion of the original page underneath, as I showed you at the end of Chapter 32.

In your HTML file create an image tag for http://www.asmarterwaytolearn.com/robo_guy.png and link it to asmarterwaytolearn.com. Save the page and display it. Click the picture.

Sample HTML code is at http://asmarterwaytolearn.com/htmlcss/practice-34-1.html.

Find the interactive coding exercises for this chapter at:
http://www.ASmarterWayToLearn.com/htmlcss/34.html

35
IMAGE MAPS PART 1

An image map is special type of clickable image. Your code sections it into two or more parts. If the user clicks one section of the image, a new page loads. If he clicks another section, a different page loads. For example, you might have a photograph showing six historical buildings in a town square. When you click on a particular building, a page loads that tells the story of the building.

Image maps require quite a bit of code, so I'm going to divide the subject into two chapters.

Let's say your image is "6-buildings.jpg." You begin with a standard **img** tag.

```
<img src="6-buildings.jpg" alt="6 historical buildings"
width="800px" height="550px">
```

Within the tag you specify the name of the image map that's going to divide up the photo into clickable regions.

```
<img src="6-buildings.jgp" alt="6 historial buildings"
width="800px" height="550px" usemap="#buildings">
```

Give the map any name you like as long as it doesn't include spaces. Precede the name with **#**.

Next you code the image map. It's a section of code that begins with an opening **map** tag and ends with a closing **/map** tag.

```
<map name="buildings">
  [Here you define each of the sections and give their
  link addresses. I'll cover this in the next chapter.]
</map>
```

Notice that the map name, "buildings," is the same name you specified in the **img** tag, but without the **#**. You've now told the browser to display the picture of the six buildings, and to connect the picture to an image map named "buildings." In the next chapter, we'll create the map itself.

Find the interactive coding exercises for this chapter at:
http://www.ASmarterWayToLearn.com/htmlcss/35.html

36
IMAGE MAPS PART 2

You've placed an image on the page, and you've connected it to an image map by writing, within the **img** tag, **usemap="#buildings"**. Then you've started an image map definition with the line…

```
<map name="buildings">
```

Here's the whole thing.

```
<map name="buildings">
<area shape="rect" alt="Tuttle House"
coords="76,42,279,510" href="tuttle-house.html">
<area shape="rect" alt="Tittle Hall"
coords="286,125,346,503" href="tittle-hall.html">
<area shape="rect" alt="Tooble Tower"
coords="352,134,445,482" href="tooble-tower.html">
<area shape="rect" alt="Tibble Manse"
coords="448,119,559,471" href="tibble-manse.html">
<area shape="rect" alt="Treble Cottage"
coords="559,211,605,466" href="treble-cottage.html">
<area shape="rect" alt="Tikkel Place"
coords="606,180,682,460" href="tikkel-place.html">
</map>
```

These are the parts of each map section.

1. The shape of the area. Write "rect" for rectangle, "circle" for circle, or "polygon" for polygon.

2. Alternative text for screen readers. You learned about this in Chapter 24.

3. The screen coordinates that define the area. See below for how to get these coordinates. Examples: For a rectangle, coordinates of 76,42,279,510 mean the clickable rectangle begins 76 pixels in from the left edge of the image and 42 pixels down from the top of the image, and extends right by 279 pixels from the left edge of the image and 510 pixels down from the top of the image. For a circle, coordinates of 100,60,10 mean the clickable circle has a center at 100 pixels in from the left edge of the image and 60 pixels down from the top of the image, and has a radius of 10 pixels. For a polygon, coordinates of 150,217,190,257,150,297,110,257 create a diamond shape. The top point of the diamond is 150 pixels in from the left edge of the image and 217 pixels down from the top of the image. The right point of the diamond is 190 pixels in from the left edge of the image and 257 pixels down from the top of the image, and so on. Three sets of coordinates create a triangle area, five sets a pentagonal area, and so on.

4. The Web address for the page to load when the user clicks the area.

Rather than trying to create an image map by hand, automate the task with a utility that does most of the work for you, including the fussy work of establishing coordinates. Web development tools like Dreamweaver include such a utility. You can also use a free online image map creator like the one at http://www.image-maps.com. My favorite tool for creating image maps is Mapedit, a downloadable program from http://www.boutell.com. There's a generous free trial period, after which you pay $15.

1. In your HTML file insert a break after the robo_guy.png image.

2. Create an image map using
   http://www.asmarterwaytolearn/stooges.jpg

3. I've mapped the Stooges' faces as three clickable areas. They're circles. The coordinates are 56,56,47…126,93,31…and 208,66,39.

4. Do a Google search for each of the Stooges. Copy the Google URLs that the searches generate and use them as the links. For example, when the user clicks Curly's face, she's taken to the Google search for Curly.

5. Save the file and display the page. Click on each of the faces.

Sample HTML code is at
http://asmarterwaytolearn.com/htmlcss/practice-36-1.html.

Find the interactive coding exercises for this chapter at:
http://www.ASmarterWayToLearn.com/htmlcss/36.html

37
BULLET LISTS AND NUMBERED LISTS

The HTML term for a bullet list is *unordered* list. *Unordered* means not numbered. An *ordered* list is a numbered list. Making bullet and numbered lists in HTML is convenient, because HTML automatically indents lists and automatically numbers ordered lists.

In both types of list, you write a tag for the list—**<ul>** for unordered lists and **<ol>** for ordered lists. Then you write a tag for each item— **<li>**, which stands for *list item*. **<li>** is the tag for individual items in either type of list, ordered or unordered.

This code creates a bullet (unordered) list.

```
<ul>
  <li>Sun</li>
  <li>Moon</li>
  <li>Planets</li>
  <li>Stars</li>
</ul>
```

This code creates a numbered (ordered) list.

```
<ol>
  <li>Wash</li>
  <li>Rinse</li>
  <li>Repeat</li>
</ol>
```

Things to notice:

- Each list item is indented two spaces.
- Each opening tag is completed with a closing tag.

In your HTML file add an unordered list and an ordered list. Save the file and display the page.

Sample HTML code is at
http://asmarterwaytolearn.com/htmlcss/practice-37-1.html.

Find the interactive coding exercises for this chapter at:
http://www.ASmarterWayToLearn.com/htmlcss/37.html

38
STYLING LISTS

Since lists are text elements, you can style them the way you'd style a paragraph or heading, with a customized font-family, font-size, font-weight, color, and margins.

This CSS code insets any unordered list, assigning extra whitespace on both the left and right.

```
ul {
  margin: 0 1.5em 0 1.5em;
}
```

You could, of course, adjust the top and/or bottom margins, too. Use the same type of code for ordered lists. Just substitute **ol** for **ul** in the code above.

The code above styles all the unordered lists on the page. You could create a class of lists, just for some of your lists.

```
ol.special {
  margin: 0 1.5em 0 1.5em;
}
```

By default, browsers don't add any space between list items. I think they look better if they're separated a bit.

```
li {
  margin: .75em;
}
```

Note that there's only one margin number in the code above. Browsers understand that it specifies the space between list items.

- This block of text is an example of default list-item indentation. The entire block is indented. This is the code if you want to specify this default style:

```
ul {
  list-style-position: outside;
}
```

- This is an example of optional list-item styling. Only the first line is indented. To specify a first-line-only indent, this is the code you would write:

```
ul {
  list-style-position: inside;
}
```

In your CSS file add space between list items. Save the file. Display the page.

Sample CSS code is at http://asmarterwaytolearn.com/htmlcss/practice-38-1.html.

Find the interactive coding exercises for this chapter at:
http://www.ASmarterWayToLearn.com/htmlcss/38.html

39
STYLING A LIST'S MARKERS

Markers are the bullets in an unordered list or the numbers in an ordered list.

If you don't specify what kind of bullets you want in an unordered list, the browser displays a disc: •

This is the CSS code that explicitly specifies a disc as the marker. It would normally be superfluous, since the disc is the default.

```
ul {
  list-style-type: disc;
}
```

To use a ○ for the bullet, substitute **circle** for **disc** in the code above.

To use a ■ substitute **square**.

You can use an image for a bullet. The example below creates a class of unordered list that uses an image.

```
ul.custom {
  list-style-image: url("images/heart.png");
}
```

In the code above, **"images/heart.png"** tells the browser the path and file name of the image.

An image used as a bullet creates headaches. To begin with, you must size the image to fit the list text. Then, if the user zooms in or out on the page, the browser doesn't adjust the bullet to fit, as it does with the built-in disc, circle, and square. Everything gets out of whack. It's possible to build a defense against this, but you're probably better off spending your coding time on something that the user cares more about.

The default list-style-type for ordered lists is **decimal**—1, 2, 3 etc. You can change it to **decimal-leading-zero**—01, 02, 03 etc.; **lower-alpha**—a, b, c etc.; **upper-alpha**—A, B, C etc.; **lower-roman**—i., ii., iii. etc.; and **upper-roman**—I, II, III etc. Here's code that creates a class for **upper-roman**.

```
ol.second-level {
  list-style-type: upper-roman;
}
```

In your CSS file style unordered list markers as squares. Save the file. Display the page.

Sample CSS code is at
http://asmarterwaytolearn.com/htmlcss/practice-39-1.html.

Find the interactive coding exercises for this chapter at:
http://www.ASmarterWayToLearn.com/htmlcss/39.html

40
MORE CSS SELECTORS

A CSS *selector* is everything on the first line that precedes the {. It's the part of a style rule that tells the browser what elements, classes, and ids a rule applies to. The selectors are highlighted in the following code fragments.

`p` {

`p.special` {

`.special` {

`p#intro` {

`#intro` {

So far you've learned to create…

1. An element selector like **p**, **div**, or **img**.
2. An element class selector like **p.special**, **div.important**, or **img.gallery**.
3. A class selector tied to no particular type of element like **.special**, **.important**, or **.gallery**.
4. An element id selector like **p#intro**, **div#sidebar**, or **img#logo**.
5. An id selector tied to no particular type of element like **#intro**, **#sidebar**, or **#logo**.

You can combine selectors to create more complicated selectors. Here's one.

`div.important p` {

The code above selects all paragraphs in a **div** that's been assigned the class "important."

The following code selects all images…that are in list items…in an unordered list…with the id "pix-list."

107

```
ul#pixList li img {
```

Here's some code that selects the first paragraph following any **div**.

```
div + p {
```

The following code selects only the first level of **div**s within the **div** that has an id of "main."

```
div#content > div {
```

So in the following code, only the highlighted **div**s are selected.

```
<div id="main">
  <div>
    <div>
      [some content]
    </div>
      [some content]
    <div>
      [some content]
    </div>
  </div>
  <div>
    [some content]
    <div>
      [some content]
    </div>
  </div>
</div>
```

You can learn a lot about selectors by playing around with the interactive W3Schools CSS selector tester at http://www.w3schools.com/CSSref/trysel.asp.

In your HTML file you coded a **div** with an id. In your CSS file double the size of all paragraphs within that **div**. Save the file. Display the page.

Sample CSS code is at http://asmarterwaytolearn.com/htmlcss/practice-40-1.html.

Find the interactive coding exercises for this chapter at:
http://www.ASmarterWayToLearn.com/htmlcss/40.html

41
TABLES: BASIC STRUCTURE

All the HTML code for a table is enclosed in an opening and closing tag.

```
<table>
  [The details of the table go here.]
</table>
```

Within those tags you create rows and columns. Here's a table with two rows and two columns.

```
<table>
  <tr>
    <td>Row 1, column 1</td>
    <td>Row 1, column 2</td>
  </tr>
  <tr>
    <td>Row 2, column 1</td>
    <td>Row 2, column 2</td>
  </tr>
</table>
```

This is what the table looks like (with a border that I added to make the rows and columns stand out).

Row 1, column 1	Row 1, column 2
Row 2, column 1	Row 2, column 2

Unless you style a border explicitly, most browsers display it without borders, like this.

Row 1, column 1   Row 1, column 2
Row 2, column 1   Row 2, column 2

You'll learn how to add borders, if you want them, in a later chapter, and to style tables so they're more attractive. For now, let's get you familiar with this barebones structure.

As you can see from the HTML code, you build a table a row at a time. You create a row using the **<tr>** (for "table row") tag. Then you create all the cells within that row using the **<td>** (for "table data") tag.

All the text content of a table cell is enclosed between the opening **<td>** tag and the closing **</td>** tag. The opening **<tr>** tag and closing **</tr>** tag don't enclose any text content. They only contain the **<td>** tags and *their* text content.

All opening tags are paired with closing tags.

Each row must have the same number of cells, created with the **<td>** and **</td>** tags, even if some of the cells are empty. To create this table, with nothing in row 2, column 1…

Apples   Oranges
         Pears

…you'd write…

```
<table>
  <tr>
    <td>Apples</td>
    <td>Oranges</td>
  </tr>
  <tr>
    <td></td>
    <td>Pears</td>
  </tr>
</table>
```

Notice that all the **<tr>** tags are indented two spaces inside the **<table>** tag, and the **<td>** tags are indented two spaces inside the **<tr>** tags.

In your HTML file code a table with two rows and two columns. Save the file. Display the page.

Sample HTML code is at http://asmarterwaytolearn.com/htmlcss/practice-41-1.html. Find the interactive coding exercises for this chapter at http://www.ASmarterWayToLearn.com/htmlcss/41.html

42
TABLES: HEADINGS

You can tell the browser to add headings for tables. Here's a table with column headings.

Dog	**Cat**
Canine	Feline
Barks	Meows
Puppy	Kitten

This is the code.

```
<table>
  <tr>
    <th scope="col">Dog</th>
    <th scope="col">Cat</th>
  </tr>
  <tr>
    <td>Canine</td>
    <td>Feline</td>
  </tr>
  <tr>
    <td>Bark</td>
    <td>Meow</td>
  </tr>
  <tr>
    <td>Puppy</td>
    <td>Kitten</td>
  </tr>
</table>
```

You begin by creating a row for the headings, just as you would for regular cells. Then, using the opening **<th>** (for "table heading") and closing **</th>** tags, you construct cells with text in them, as you would for regular text cells. But note **scope="col"**. This tells the browser that you want column headings—headings on top—not row headings, which would begin each row on the left.

By default, most browsers bold heading text and center it

horizontally with the cell.

Now let's create a table with row headings, like this one.

Species	Canine	Feline
Sound	Bark	Meow
Immature	Puppy	Kitten

This is the code.

```
<table>
  <tr>
    <th scope="row">Species</th>
    <td>Canine</td>
    <td>Feline</td>
  </tr>
  <tr>
    <th scope="row">Sound</th>
    <td>Bark</td>
    <td>Meow</td>
  </tr>
  <tr>
    <th scope="row">Immature</th>
    <td>Puppy</td>
    <td>Kitten</td>
  </tr>
</table>
```

You create a heading for each row. And you write **scope="row"**. Here's the table with both column and row headings.

	Dog	**Cat**
Species	Canine	Feline
Sound	Bark	Meow
Immature	Puppy	Kitten

This is the code.

```
<table>
  <tr>
    <th scope="col"></th>
    <th scope="col">Dog</th>
    <th scope="col">Cat</th>
  </tr>
  <tr>
    <th scope="row">Species</th>
    <td>Canine</td>
    <td>Feline</td>
  </tr>
  <tr>
    <th scope="row">Sound</th>
    <td>Bark</td>
    <td>Meow</td>
  </tr>
  <tr>
    <th scope="row">Immature</th>
    <td>Puppy</td>
    <td>Kitten</td>
  </tr>
</table>
```

Notice that there are three column headings, the first one blank. This tells the browser that there is no column heading over the column of row headings.

In your HTML file code a table with both column and row headings. Save the file. Display the page.

Sample HTML code is at
http://asmarterwaytolearn.com/htmlcss/practice-42-1.html.

Find the interactive coding exercises for this chapter at:
http://www.ASmarterWayToLearn.com/htmlcss/42.html

43
TABLES: SPANNING COLUMNS AND ROWS

Sometimes you need to combine two or more cells into a single, extra-wide cell.

	1 pm	2pm	3pm
Gym	Dodge ball	Kick boxing	Sack racing
Exercise Room	Spinning	Yoga marathon	
Pool	Water polo		

The table above shows the early-afternoon schedule for three facilities. I've added borders, and I've highlighted the two spanned rows that I want you to pay attention to. Neither the borders nor the highlighting are part of the code below. You'll learn how to add both kinds of styling in subsequent chapters. This is the code.

```
<table>
  <tr>
    <th scope="col"></th>
    <th scope="col">1 pm</th>
    <th scope="col">2 pm</th>
    <th scope="col">3 pm</th>
  </tr>
  <tr>
    <th scope="row">Gym</th>
    <td>Dodge ball</td>
    <td>Kick boxing</td>
    <td>Sack racing</td>
  </tr>
  <tr>
    <th scope="row">Exercise room</th>
    <td>Spinning</td>
    <td colspan="2">Yoga marathon</td>
  <tr>
    <th scope="row">Pool</th>
    <td colspan="3">Water polo</td>
  </tr>
</table>
```

The code for a column-span cell looks like a regular **<td>** cell, except for the code **colspan="[*number of columns to span*]"**. The closing tag is the same as for a regular **<td>** cell.

Notice that a **<td>** with the **colspan** feature replaces the same number of regular **<td>**s as the number of columns that are spanned. In the first row, there are three regular **<td>**s. In the second row, where two columns are spanned, there's one regular **<td>** plus the span. In the third row, where three columns are spanned, there's no regular **<td>**.

You can make table headings span columns, too. The code is…

```
<th scope="row" colspan="[number of columns to
span]">Whatever</th>
```

Spanning rows works the same way as spanning columns, but uses **rowspan**.

Here's the table above, reconfigured so the facilities are at the top and the times are on the left.

	Gym	Exercise Room	Pool
1 pm	Dodge ball	Spinning	
2 pm	Kick boxing	Yoga marathon	Water polo
3 pm	Sack racing		

This is the code.

```
<table>
  <tr>
    <th scope="col"></th>
    <th scope="col">Gym</th>
    <th scope="col">Exercise Room</th>
    <th scope="col">Pool</th>
  </tr>
  <tr>
    <th scope="row">1 pm</th>
    <td>Dodge ball</td>
    <td>Spinning</td>
    <td rowspan="3">Water polo</td>
  </tr>
  <tr>
    <th scope="row">2 pm</th>
    <td>Spinning</td>
    <td rowspan="2">Yoga marathon</td>
  <tr>
    <th scope="row">3 pm</th>
    <td rowspan="3">Sack racing</td>
  </tr>
</table>
```

You can make table headings span rows, too. The code is…

```
<th scope="column" rowspan="[number of rows to
span]">Whatever</th>
```

You can divide a table into three sections: a header, body, and footer. This helps screen readers, but doesn't do anything for sighted users that you can't do using the code I've already taught you. I'll show you an example. You won't be tested on it in the exercises.

	Gym	Exercise Room	Pool
1 pm	Dodge ball	Spinning	
2 pm	Kick boxing	Yoga marathon	Water polo
3 pm	Sack racing		
	3 activities	2 activities	1 activity

This is the code.

```
<table>
  <thead>
    <tr>
      <th></th>
      <th>Gym</th>
      <th>Exercise Room</th>
      <th>Pool</th>
    </tr>
  </thead>
  <tfoot>
    <tr>
      <th></th>
      <th>3 activities</th>
      <th>2 activities</th>
      <th>1 activity</th>
    </tr>
  </tfoot>
  <tbody>
    <tr>
      <th scope="row">1 pm</th>
      <td>Dodge ball</td>
      <td>Spinning</td>
      <td rowspan="3">Water polo</td>
    </tr>
    <tr>
      <th scope="row">2 pm</th>
      <td>Spinning</td>
      <td rowspan="2">Yoga marathon</td>
    <tr>
      <th scope="row">3 pm</th>
      <td rowspan="3">Sack racing</td>
    </tr>
  </tbody>
</table>
```

Code a simple table with two rows and two columns. In the second row, span the columns.

Sample HTML code is at
http://asmarterwaytolearn.com/htmlcss/practice-43-1.html.

Find the interactive coding exercises for this chapter at:
http://www.ASmarterWayToLearn.com/htmlcss/43.html

44
TABLES: BORDERS

You can create a table with borders or without.

Here's a table where all the cells have borders.

	Gym	Exercise Room	Pool
1 pm	Dodge ball	Spinning	
2 pm	Kick boxing	Yoga marathon	Water polo
3 pm	Sack racing		

This is the CSS code.

```
th, td {
  border: 1px solid black;
}
```

By specifying **1px solid black** I'm asking for a solid black line of minimal—1-pixel—width. For a heavier line, increase the pixel number. For another type of line, specify **dotted** or one of the other border styles covered in Chapter 17.

By default, browsers add a little space between cells, as in the table shown above. This creates gaps between the hairline borders. If you don't want those gaps, add a specification for the table:

```
table {
  border-collapse: collapse;
}
```

This is the result.

	Gym	Exercise Room	Pool
1 pm	Dodge ball	Spinning	
2 pm	Kick boxing	Yoga marathon	Water polo
3 pm	Sack racing		

By default, browsers don't draw a border around anything. If you don't want borders, there's nothing to code. But with CSS you can add borders anywhere you like. For example, here's a table with top and bottom borders framing the table headers.

	Gym	Exercise Room	Pool
1 pm	Dodge ball	Spinning	
2 pm	Kick boxing	Yoga marathon	Water polo
3 pm	Sack racing		

Here's the CSS code.

```
th.top-row {
  border-top: 1px solid black;
  border-bottom: 1px solid black;
}
```

The first seven lines of HTML would be…

```
<table>
  <tr>
    <th class="top-row" scope="col"></th>
    <th class="top-row" scope="col">Gym</th>
    <th class="top-row" scope="col">Exercise Room</th>
    <th class="top-row" scope="col">Pool</th>
  </tr>
  [etc.]
```

The only reason I have to define a special class of **<th>** is that I've also got **<th>**s running down the left side of the table, denoting times. Since I don't want borders on these, I need to make a distinction for **<th>**s that have column scope. Otherwise, I could just write…

```
th {
  border-top: 1px solid black;
  border-bottom: 1px solid black;
}
```

To create left and right borders use **border-left** and **border-right**. For example, suppose you want heavy orange borders defining the left and right edges of certain tables.

	Gym	Exercise Room	Pool
1 pm	Dodge ball	Spinning	
2 pm	Kick boxing	Yoga marathon	Water polo
3 pm	Sack racing		

This is the code.

```
table.standout {
  border-left: 5px solid orange;
  border-right: 5px solid orange;
}
```

The first line of HTML would be…

```
<table class="standout">
```

In your CSS file specify borders for all cells. Eliminate space between borders. Save the file. Display the page.

Sample CSS code is at
http://asmarterwaytolearn.com/htmlcss/practice-44-1.html.

Find the interactive coding exercises for this chapter at:
http://www.ASmarterWayToLearn.com/htmlcss/44.html

45
TABLES: SPACING PART 1

Browsers don't add breathing room between the table cell borders and the text inside. They're jammed up against each other. It looks crowded.

Row 1, column 1	Row 1, column 2
Row 2, column 1	Row 2, column 2

The solution is to add *padding*.

```
th, td {
  padding: .25em;
}
```

The CSS code above adds a little whitespace all around the text.

Row 1, column 1	Row 1, column 2
Row 2, column 1	Row 2, column 2

You adjust the amount of padding by changing the **em** number. You can specify different padding for different sides.

```
td {
  padding: .25em 1.5em 0 1.5em;
}
```

The CSS code above adds extra padding at the top, just a little on the sides, and none on the bottom. The numbers start at the top and proceed clockwise. To specify none, write **0**, not **0em**. To space cells apart—say, even farther apart than the browser default. Here's the CSS code. I'm going to specify large spaces, so they're easy to see.

```
table {
  border-spacing: 1em;
}
```

This is the result.

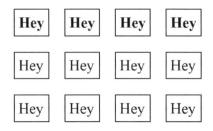

Note that border-spacing is something you specify for the whole table, not the **<th>** or **<td>** elements.

As usual, you can specify different border-spacing for different sides.

```
table {
  border-spacing: 0 .25em 0 .25em;
}
```

The above CSS code would add extra space on the left and right and leave top and bottom space at the default width.

Even if a table doesn't have borders, you can use border-spacing to add whitespace between the cells. Here's the same table, with no border specified but with the all-around border-spacing of **2.5em**.

Hey	Hey	Hey	Hey
Hey	Hey	Hey	Hey
Hey	Hey	Hey	Hey

In your CSS file add .25em of padding to all cells. Save the file. Display the page. Sample CSS code is at http://asmarterwaytolearn.com/htmlcss/practice-45-1.html.

Find the interactive coding exercises for this chapter at:
http://www.ASmarterWayToLearn.com/htmlcss/45.html

46
TABLES: SPACING PART 2

By default, browsers adjust cell size to contents. If you write...

```
<table>
  <tr>
    <th>Monday</th>
    <th>Tuesday</th>
    <th>Wednesday</th>
    <th>Thursday</th>
    <th>Friday</th>
  </tr>
  <tr>
    <td>Rome</td>
    <td>Addis Ababa</td>
    <td>Cairo</td>
    <td>Saint Seabury on the Thames</td>
    <td>Dublin</td>
  </tr>
</table>
```

...the browser displays this...(I've styled it with a border and padding and collapsed the spaces between cells.)

Monday	Tuesday	Wednesday	Thursday	Friday
Rome	Addis Ababa	Cairo	Saint Seabury on the Thames	Dublin

The browser has used space efficiently, assigning just enough width to fit everything in. I think this looks better:

Monday	Tuesday	Wednesday	Thursday	Friday
Rome	Addis Ababa	Cairo	Saint Seabury on the Thames	Dublin

Instead of letting the browser allocate space on the basis of need, I styled the cells so they'd all be 20% of the width of the full table. In other words, they'd all be the same width.

```
th, td {
    border: 1px solid black;
    padding: 5px;
    width: 20%;
}
```

When I specify cell width instead of letting the browser allocate space based on content, I force the browser to automatically wrap longer text lines so they fit into my chosen width.

I could, if I wanted to, define some CSS classes or ids to make different cells different widths.

Next point: I'm not sure I want the table to be so big. So I'll force the browser to give me a narrower table by specifying *its* width as less than 100%. I'll tell it to make it three-quarters the width of the window or **div** that it sits in.

```
table {
    width:75%;
}
```

This is the result.

Monday	Tuesday	Wednesday	Thursday	Friday
Rome	Addis Ababa	Cairo	Saint Seabury on the Thames	Dublin

Notice that the browser automatically wraps longer lines into multiple lines to fit them into the width.

1. In your HTML file code a simple table with two rows and two columns. Give it an id.

2. In your CSS file reduce the table's width to a fraction of the window's width.

3. Make the two rows equal.

Sample HTML code is at http://asmarterwaytolearn.com/htmlcss/practice-46-1.html. Sample CSS code is at http://asmarterwaytolearn.com/htmlcss/practice-46-2.html.

Find the interactive coding exercises for this chapter at:
http://www.ASmarterWayToLearn.com/htmlcss/46.html

47
TABLES: ALIGNING TEXT

In Chapter 14 you learned to align text on the page using…
```
text-align: left;
text-align: right;
text-align: center;
text-align: justify;
```
You can use this same code to align text in table cells. For example, you can write…

```
table {
  text-align: left
}
```

The text in all cells, including **<th>** cells, will be positioned on the left of the cell. (The text in **<td>** cells would have been positioned on the left anyway, by default.)

You can be more surgical by styling, say, just **<th>** or **<td>** cells. For example, you know that by default, browsers set text in **<td>** cells on the left. If you'd prefer to center the text, you could write…

```
td {
  text-align: center;
}
```

Monday	Tuesday	Wednesday	Thursday	Friday
Rome	Addis Ababa	Cairo	Saint Seabury on the Thames	Dublin

If you have a column of numbers, you might want to set them to the right. You'd create a class of **<td>** to do that.

```
td.num {
  text-align: right;
}
```

You can also control the vertical alignment within cells, using…

```
vertical-align: top;
vertical-align: bottom;
vertical-align: center;
```

You can't specify vertical alignment for the whole table, only for **<th>** and **<td>** elements. You can, of course, create classes of **<th>** and **<td>** elements that have their own alignment.

By default, text is vertically centered in both **<th>** and **<td>** cells. If you wanted **<th>** text moved to the bottom of the cell, you could write.

```
th {
  vertical-align: bottom;
}
```

This code would move the text to the top…

```
th {
  vertical-align: top;
}
```

In your CSS file center text in the cells of the most recent table, the one with the id. Save the file. Display the page.

Sample CSS code is at

http://asmarterwaytolearn.com/htmlcss/practice-47-1.html.

Find the interactive coding exercises for this chapter at:
http://www.ASmarterWayToLearn.com/htmlcss/47.html

48
TABLES: BACKGROUND-COLOR

You can use code you learned in earlier chapters to style the text for an entire table, for **<th>** and **<td>** elements, and for classes and ids of any of these elements.

For example:

```
th, td {
  font-family: Georgia, "Times New Roman", Times, serif;
  font-size: 1.5em;
  font-weight: 900;
  color: gray;
  letter-spacing: .1em;
}
```

This what the table would look like.

Monday	Tuesday	Wednesday	Thursday	Friday
Rome	Addis Ababa	Cairo	Saint Seabury on the Thames	Dublin

A characteristic that can be especially useful in tables is background-color. For example you can use it to shade alternative rows to make reading a row easier.

Start by defining a class of <tr> and specifying, let's say, lightgray as the background-color.

```
tr.even-row {
  background-color: lightgray;
}
```

You'd write the HTML like this.

```
<table>
   <tr>
     <th scope="col">Product</th>
     <th scope="col">Price</th>
     <th scope="col">Shipping</th>
     <th scope="col">Tax</th>
    <th scope="col">Total</th>
   </tr>
   <tr>
     <td>Swisher</td>
     <td>76.75</td>
     <td>6.50</td>
     <td>.83</td>
     <td>83.93</td>
   </tr>
   <tr class="even-row">
     <td>Stirrer</td>
     <td>106.60</td>
     <td>8.00</td>
     <td>1.33</td>
     <td>115.93</td>
   </tr>
   <tr>
     <td>Shaker</td>
     <td>31.50</td>
     <td>2.90</td>
     <td>.33</td>
     <td>34.37</td>
   </tr>
   <tr class="even-row">
     <td>Swirler</td>
     <td>220.00</td>
     <td>14.00</td>
     <td>2.60</td>
     <td>236.60</td>
   </tr>
   <tr>
     <td>Splasher</td>
     <td>89.00</td>
     <td>6.50</td>
     <td>.91</td>
     <td>96.41</td>
   </tr>
</table>
```

With some additional styling I'm not showing you here, the table would look like this.

Product	Price	Shipping	Tax	Total
Swisher	76.75	6.50	.83	83.93
Stirrer	106.60	8.00	1.33	115.93
Shaker	31.50	2.90	.33	34.37
Swirler	220.00	14.00	2.60	236.60
Splasher	89.00	6.50	.91	96.41

1. In your HTML file revise the most recent table, the one with an id. Assign a class to the second row. Save the file.

2. In your CSS file code a light background color for that class. Save the file.

3. Display the page.

Sample HTML code is at http://asmarterwaytolearn.com/htmlcss/practice-48-1.html. Sample CSS code is at http://asmarterwaytolearn.com/htmlcss/practice-48-2.html.

Find the interactive coding exercises for this chapter at:
http://www.ASmarterWayToLearn.com/htmlcss/48.html

49
FORMS: THE FORM TAG

It's a rare website that doesn't use some forms. At a minimum, you're probably going to want to include an email form on your site to make it easy for users to contact you.

Every form begins and ends with an opening **<form>** and closing **</form>** tag.

`<form>` `action="send-email.php" method="post">`

  [Here's where the contents of the form, like input fields and a submit button, are coded. We'll start working on these in the next chapter.]

`</form>`

In most cases, when a user completes a form, a program separate from the HTML file runs. In the example above, **action="send-email.php"** tells the browser that when the user submits the form, the information the user has entered in the form is to be sent to a PHP program on the website for processing. The program's URL is "send-email.php." It's a program that runs on the host's server. This is different from an HTML file. An HTML file is *stored* on the host's server but *runs* in the user's browser.

In the case of the example, **send-email.php** might send an email to the site owner that includes the data the user has entered. Or a program might write the data entered by the user to a database on the server. Or a program might process credit card information entered in a form.

There are all kinds of programs, written in various languages, that can process data from a form. The languages include PHP, Ruby, Python, Perl, Java, and C#. The processing programs written in these languages are outside the scope of this book, so you won't learn anything about processing forms here, other than learning how to specify the form action in HTML tags.

But don't be discouraged if you don't know any of these languages.

At sites like http://www.hotscripts.com/ you'll find thousands of programs, both free and for sale, that process forms for every purpose. You don't need to know a computer language to use these scripts. The people who write them tell you how to change a few lines of the code to adapt them so they'll work on your site. Make a few simple changes, then upload the code to your site, and you're in business.

The example above specifies **`method="post"`**. This method is the one you use to process more than a little bit of information, and when you want to keep the information secure. The second method, **`get`**, is used mostly for search forms. You know a form is using the **`get`** method when the information entered in the form (connected by plus signs) appears in the URL after you click **Submit**. Here's the URL that displayed when I searched the New Yorker site for "alice munro."

http://www.newyorker.com/search?qt=dismax&sort=score+desc&query=**alice+munro**&submit=

If you don't specify a method, the **`get`** method is used. Since this unsecure method isn't appropriate for most purposes, you'll usually want to specify the **`post`** method.

Find the interactive coding exercises for this chapter at:
http://www.ASmarterWayToLearn.com/htmlcss/49.html

50
FORMS: TEXT INPUT

Here's a form that's limited to one single-line text field. It's useless, because it doesn't include a **Submit** button. We'll add that later.

Last name: [_____]

This is the HTML.

```
<form action="send-email.php" method="post">
  Last name:
  <input type="text" name="surname" size="25"
maxlength="40">
</form>
```

It begins with some plain text, **Last name:** It doesn't have to be placed to the left of the field. It could be above, to the right, or even below the field.

The **input** tag has four parts:

1. **type="text"**. This tells the browser to display a single-line box in which the user can enter text.

2. **name="surname"**. The name can be almost anything you like, but don't use spaces in it. The name tells the program that's processing the data what to call the information that the user enters in that field.

3. **size="25"**. This tells the browser how wide to make the box. When you write **size="25"** you're telling the browser to make the box roughly 25 characters wide. If the user types more than 25 characters, the line will scroll horizontally. Specifying the size is optional. If you don't specify it, the browser will make a text box 20 characters wide by default.

4. **maxlength="40"**. This tells the browser to put a limit on the number of characters that can be typed into this field. If there's scrolling, the scrolling will stop at this limit. Specifying the

maximum length is optional. If you don't specify it, the box will accept any number of characters and will scroll as far as it needs to in order to accommodate all the characters.

A password field is like a text input field, except that the characters that the user enters are disguised as asterisks or circles in the field. You code a password field the same way you code a text input field, except that you replace the world **"text"** with the word **"password"**.

```
<input type="password" name="pass" size="20"
maxlength="40">
```

All of the individual parts of a form—the one-line text box that you just learned to create and all the rest that you're about to learn—are called *controls*.

Code a form with a single text input. Don't bother with the action or method. Specify name, size, and maxlength. Save the file. Display the page.

Sample HTML code is at http://asmarterwaytolearn.com/htmlcss/practice-50-1.html.

Find the interactive coding exercises for this chapter at:
http://www.ASmarterWayToLearn.com/htmlcss/50.html

51
FORMS: TEXTAREA

In the last chapter you learned how to code a one-line text box using **input type="text"**. Here's a second type of control, a multi-line text box. (In this example form I haven't included a first-name field. This example form is only for learning, so we'll limit it to just one control of each type.)

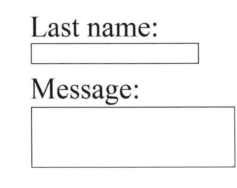

Last name:

Message:

This is the HTML.

```
<form action="send-email.php" method="post">
  Last name:
  <br>
  <input type="text" name="surname" size="25"
maxlength="40">
  <br><br>
  Message:
  <br>
  <textarea name="message" rows="4" cols="30"></textarea>
</form>
```

Notice, first, that this tag is closed, with **</textarea>**.

rows="8" cols="30" specifies the number of visible rows and columns. By default, entered text will scroll if the user types beyond the specified number of rows. By default, the field can be resized by the user when she drags the lower-right corner with the mouse.

In your HTML file add a text area to the form you've already coded. Specify rows and columns. Save the file. Display the page.

Sample HTML code is at
http://asmarterwaytolearn.com/htmlcss/practice-51-1.html.

Find the interactive coding exercises for this chapter at:
http://www.ASmarterWayToLearn.com/htmlcss/51.html

52
FORMS: SUBMIT

Let's add a submit button to the form. When the user clicks it, the form is submitted. That is, all the data is sent to the program (PHP or another language) that processes it.

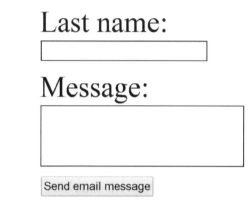

This is the code.

```
<form action="send-email.php" method="post">
  Last name:
  <br>
  <input type="text" name="surname"
size="25"maxlength="40">
  <br><br>
  Message:
  <br>
  <textarea name="message" rows="4" cols="30"></textarea>
  <br><br>
  <input type="submit" value="Send email message">
</form>
```

This is a simple input tag, with only two parts. The first part creates the button that, when clicked, submits the form:

```
input type="submit"
```

The second part specifies the button text. Instead of "Send email message," it could be "Submit," "Send," "Subscribe," "Purchase," or any other text you want…

```
value="Send email message"
```

The **submit** tag creates a standard button. If you want a custom button, create your own button image and write a tag like this.

```
<input type="image" src="images/subscribe-button.png"
alt="Sign up" width="72" height="18">
```

The browser knows this is a **Submit** button even though you say the input type is **"image"**. Everything you write after **<input type="image"** is exactly the same as the **img** tag you learned to write in Chapter 24.

In your HTML file add a **Submit** button to the form you've already created. Save the file. Display the page.

Sample HTML code is at http://asmarterwaytolearn.com/htmlcss/practice-52-1.html.

Find the interactive coding exercises for this chapter at:
http://www.ASmarterWayToLearn.com/htmlcss/52.html

53
FORMS: RADIO BUTTONS

Now we'll add *radio buttons* to the form. Radio buttons allow the user to make one and only one selection. We'll ask the user to tell us how she found our site.

Last name:

How did you find us?

◉ Google ○ Review ○ Friend

Message:

Send email message

This is the code.

```
<form action="send-email.php" method="post">
  Last name:
  <br>
  <input type="text" name="surname"
size="25"maxlength="40">
  <br><br>
  How did you find us?<br>
  <input type="radio" name="found-thru" value="Google"
checked="checked"> Google
  <input type="radio" name="found-thru" value="Review">
Review
  <input type="radio" name="found-thru" value="Friend">
Friend
  <br><br>
  Message:
  <br>
  <textarea name="message" rows="4" cols="30"></textarea>
  <br><br>
  <input type="submit" value="Send email message">
</form>
```

Notice that each radio button has its own separate **input** tag. What binds all the radio buttons in a group together is that they're all given the same name. In the example, I've given it the name "found-thru."

It begins as other **input** tags do, but specifies "radio" instead of "text," "submit," or another input type...

```
input type="radio"
```

The name, shared by all the radio buttons in a particular radio button group, binds all the buttons within the group together. You make up the name...

```
name="found-thru"
```

The value is the word or words sent to the processing program telling the program which button has been checked.

```
value="Google"
```

The next part is optional. When you include it in a tag, it means the button is checked by default. Since only one button in a group can be checked, you would include this in only one button tag within a group. If you omit it, no button is checked by default.

```
checked="checked"
```

Finally, there's the text that the user sees. It would normally be the same word or words that you specify for **value**.

Google

In your HTML file add two radio buttons to the form you've already coded. Save the file. Display the page.
Sample HTML code is at
http://asmarterwaytolearn.com/htmlcss/practice-53-1.html.

Find the interactive coding exercises for this chapter at:
http://www.ASmarterWayToLearn.com/htmlcss/53.html

54
FORMS: CHECKBOXES

Checkboxes work like radio buttons, except that the user can check more than one. Let's add checkboxes that allow the user to give us some feedback.

Last name:

[   ]

How did you find us?

◉ Google ○ Review ○ Friend

How would you describe our site?

☑ Wonderful ▪ Fabulous ▪ Brilliant

Message:

[   ]

[Send email message]

This is the code.

```
<form action="send-email.php" method="post">
  Last name:
  <br>
  <input type="text" name="surname"
size="25"maxlength="40">
  <br><br>
  How did you find us?<br>
  <input type="radio" name="found-thru" value="Google"
checked="checked"> Google
  <input type="radio" name="found-thru" value="Review">
Review
  <input type="radio" name="found-thru" value="Friend">
Friend
  <br><br>
  How would you describe our site?<br>
  <input type="checkbox" name="feedback" value="Wonderful"
checked="checked"> Wonderful
  <input type="checkbox" name="feedback" value="Fabulous">
Fabulous
  <input type="checkbox" name="feedback" value="Brilliant">
Brilliant
  <br><br>
  Message:
  <br>
  <textarea name="message" rows="4" cols="30"></textarea>
  <br><br>
  <input type="submit" value="Send email message">
</form>
```

Again, as with radio buttons, each checkbox has its own separate **input** tag. And again, what binds all the checkboxes in a group together is that they're all given the same name. In the example, the name is "feedback."

You're familiar with the beginning part by now.

```
input type="checkbox"
```

The name, shared by all the checkboxes in a particular checkbox group, binds all the checkboxes within the group together. You make up the name.

```
name="feedback"
```

The value is the word or words sent to the processing program telling the program that this box has been checked.

```
value="Wonderful"
```

The next part is optional. When you include it in a tag, it means the box is checked by default. You can use this specification to pre-check as many boxes as you like. If you omit it from all checkbox tags, no box is pre-checked.

```
checked="checked"
```

Finally, there's the text that the user sees. It would normally be the same word or words that you specify for **value**.

```
Wonderful
```

In your HTML file add two checkboxes to the form you've already coded. Save the file. Display the page.
Sample HTML code is at
http://asmarterwaytolearn.com/htmlcss/practice-54-1.html.

Find the interactive coding exercises for this chapter at:
http://www.ASmarterWayToLearn.com/htmlcss/54.html

55
FORMS: SELECT BOX

The standard way to ask the user to tell you the state he lives in is the *select box*. A select box works well when you want the user to select from a list that's too long to be handled gracefully by radio buttons. Like radio buttons, only one selection can be made in a select box.

Let's add one for a state selection. I'll just do three states to show you how it works.

Last name:

How did you find us?
⦿ Google ◦ Review ◦ Friend

How would you describe our site?
☑ Wonderful ☐ Fabulous ☐ Brilliant

Your state:

Alabama ⬍

Message:

Send email message

This is the code.

```
<form action="send-email.php" method="post">
  Last name:
  <br>
  <input type="text" name="surname"
size="25"maxlength="40">
  <br><br>
  How did you find us?<br>
  <input type="radio" name="found-thru" value="Google"
checked="checked"> Google
  <input type="radio" name="found-thru" value="Review">
Review
  <input type="radio" name="found-thru" value="Friend">
Friend
  <br><br>
  How would you describe our site?<br>
  <input type="checkbox" name="feedback" value="Wonderful"
checked="checked"> Wonderful
  <input type="checkbox" name="feedback" value="Fabulous">
Fabulous
  <input type="checkbox" name="feedback" value="Brilliant">
Brilliant
  <br><br>
Your state:<br>
<select name="current-state">
  <option value="AL">Alabama</option>
  <option value="AK">Alaska</option>
  <option value="AZ">Arizona</option>
</select>
<br><br>
  Message:
  <br>
  <textarea name="message" rows="4" cols="30"></textarea>
  <br><br>
  <input type="submit" value="Send email message">
</form>
```

The syntax for a select box is different than the syntax you've learned for other input types.

- Starts with **<select**, not **<input type=**

- Unlike radio buttons and checkboxes, which are freestanding and bound together by a common name, all the choices are enclosed by opening and closing **select** tags.

- Unlike most other input types, **option** tags are closed.

- The **name** is specified only once, in the **select** tag.

By default, the first option is pre-selected. In the example, it's Alabama. You can pre-select another option by including in one of the **option** tags the words **select="selected"**.

A problem with the example is that if the user doesn't bother to make a selection, his state will be input as Alabama even if he lives in Alaska, since Alabama defaults as the choice if the user doesn't make one. The solution is to make the first option something like "Select a state." When the user clicks the input button, a little JavaScript routine can check to see whether "Select a state" is the selected option, which means that the user hasn't made a selection. If so, the user can be prompted to select a state. My book *A Smarter Way to Learn JavaScript*, available at Amazon, shows you how to write this routine.

In your HTML file add a select box with two selections to the form you've already coded. Save the file. Display the page.

Sample HTML code is at http://asmarterwaytolearn.com/htmlcss/practice-55-1.html.

Find the interactive coding exercises for this chapter at:
http://www.ASmarterWayToLearn.com/htmlcss/55.html

56
FORMS: LABEL

It's a good idea to give each control a **label** tag. The **form** tag itself doesn't take one, but it's a good idea to add one to each text field, text area, radio button, checkbox, and selection option. But it isn't required.

Labels allow screen readers to call out the text that goes with each control.

For example, if the user is working with a screen reader and you're got a one-line text box for the user's last name, the **label** tag makes the screen reader say, "Last name" when the user tabs to the field.

In addition to making the text readable by a screen reader, a label makes the text clickable like the control itself, giving the user a bigger target. This is especially helpful for radio buttons and boxes, which can be hard to hit with the cursor. For example, if you write...

```
<label><input type="radio" name="found-thru"
value="Google">Google</label>
```

...the user doesn't have to hit the button. He can click "Google" and the button will be checked.

Notice how the label tag encloses both the text and the control. This is the easy way to add a label tag. The hard way, preferred by experts for esoteric reasons, requires that you give the control an id. In this method, the opening and closing label tags enclose only the text.

```
<input type="radio" name="found-thru" id="goo"
value="Google"><label for="goo">Google</label>
```

In your HTML file use the easy way to add labels to the radio buttons. Use the hard way to add labels to the checkbox buttons. Save the file. Display the page.

Sample HTML code is at http://asmarterwaytolearn.com/htmlcss/practice-56-1.html.

Find the interactive coding exercises for this chapter at:
http://www.ASmarterWayToLearn.com/htmlcss/56.html

57
GROUPING RELATED ELEMENTS

If your form has a lot of parts, you can improve the user's experience by grouping related parts together visually. Take this form...

First name: [_____] Last name: [_____]

Email: [_____]

What is the meaning of life?

[_____]

What do you want on your pizza?
▫Pepperoni ▫Sausage ▫Mushrooms ▫Olives

It'll be easier for the user to understand if you enclose each group in a box...

First name: [_____] Last name: [_____]
Email: [_____]

What is the meaning of life?

[_____]

What do you want on your pizza?
▪Pepperoni ▪Sausage ▪Mushrooms ▪Olives

This is the code. (I've added a little CSS styling. We won't go into that now.)

```
<form action="questionnaire.php" method="post">
  <fieldset>
    <label>First name: <input type="text" name="first-name"
size="15" maxlength="30"></label>
    <label>Last name: <input type="text" name="last-name"
size="15" maxlength="30"></label><br><br>
    <label>Email: <input type="text" name="email" size="25"
maxlength="40"></label>
  </fieldset>
  <br>
  <fieldset>
    <label>What is the meaning of life?<br><textarea
name="meaning" rows="4"
cols="40"></textarea></label><br><br>
    What do you want on your pizza?<br>
    <label><input type="checkbox" name="topping">Pepperoni
</label>
    <label><input type="checkbox" name="topping">Sausage
</label>
    <label><input type="checkbox" name="topping">Mushrooms
</label>
    <label><input type="checkbox" name="topping">Olives
</label>
  </fieldset>
</form>
```

By enclosing the two groups of controls in opening and closing **fieldset** tags, we tell the browser to enclose the groups in separate boxes.

Note that everything within the **fieldset** tags is indented 2 spaces.

We can improve the readability of the form even further by adding *legends*—descriptive text that's at the top of the box.

```
┌─Contact info ────────────────────────────────┐
│ First name: [          ]  Last name: [          ] │
│                                               │
│ Email: [              ]                        │
└───────────────────────────────────────────────┘

┌─Questions ───────────────────────────────────┐
│ What is the meaning of life?                   │
│ ┌─────────────────────┐                        │
│ │                     │                        │
│ │                     │                        │
│ └─────────────────────┘                        │
│                                               │
│ What do you want on your pizza?                │
│ ▧Pepperoni ▧Sausage ▧Mushrooms ▧Olives         │
└───────────────────────────────────────────────┘
```

Now the first group has the legend "Contact info" and the second group has the legend "Questions."

This is the code.

```
<form action="questionnaire.php" method="post">
  <fieldset>
    <legend>Contact info</legend>
    <label>First name: <input type="text" name="first-name"
size="15" maxlength="30"></label>
    <label>Last name: <input type="text" name="last-name"
size="15" maxlength="30"></label><br><br>
    <label>Email: <input type="text" name="email" size="25"
maxlength="40"></label>
  </fieldset>
  <br>
  <fieldset>
    <legend>Questions</legend>
    <label>What is the meaning of life?<br><textarea
name="meaning" rows="4"
cols="40"></textarea></label><br><br>
    What do you want on your pizza?<br>
    <label>Pepperoni<input type="checkbox"
name="topping"></label>
    <label>Sausage<input type="checkbox"
name="topping"></label>
    <label>Mushrooms<input type="checkbox"
name="topping"></label>
    <label>Olives<input type="checkbox"
name="topping"></label>
  </fieldset>
</form>
```

The **legend** tags go on the line following the opening **fieldset** tag and, like everything enclosed by the **fieldset** tags, are indented 2 spaces.

In your HTML group the two text fields with one set of **fieldset** tags and the radio, checkbox, and selection controls with a second set of **fieldset** tags. Make up legends for both groups. Save the file. Display the page.

Sample HTML code is at http://asmarterwaytolearn.com/htmlcss/practice-57-1.html.

Find the interactive coding exercises for this chapter at:
http://www.ASmarterWayToLearn.com/htmlcss/57.html

58
FORMS: STYLING

Here's a filled-out form without any CSS styling.

```
┌─ Contact info ──────────────────────────────┐
│ First name: [Mark    ]  Last name: [Myers    ]│
│                                              │
│ Email: [mark@asmarterwaytolearn.com]         │
└──────────────────────────────────────────────┘

┌─ Question ──────────────────────────────────┐
│ What's new?                                  │
│  ┌────────────────────────────────┐          │
│  │ I have a new book coming out that│          │
│  │ helps you learn it faster and   │          │
│  │ remember it longer.             │          │
│  └────────────────────────────────┘          │
└──────────────────────────────────────────────┘
[Send message]
```

Now I'll give it some styling. It isn't museum-quality, but I like it better.

```
┌─Contact info ───────────────────────────┐
│ First name: [Mark      ]                 │
│                                          │
│ Last name: [Myers       ]                │
│                                          │
│ Email:                                   │
│ [mark@asmarterwaytolearn.com]            │
└──────────────────────────────────────────┘

┌─Question ───────────────────────────────┐
│ What's new?                              │
│ ┌──────────────────────────────────────┐ │
│ │ I have a new book coming out that    │ │
│ │ helps you learn it faster and        │ │
│ │ remember it longer.                  │ │
│ └──────────────────────────────────────┘ │
└──────────────────────────────────────────┘

[ Send message ]
```

163

There are more ways to customize HTML forms than there are stars in the galaxy. Let me show you the minimal styling I used for the form shown above.

To begin with, I styled the labels and legends by specifying a sans serif font-family and larger font-size for the form.

```
form {
  width: 50%;
  margin: 0 auto 0 auto;
  font-family: Verdana, Geneva, sans-serif;
  font-size: 1em;
}
```

The styling shown above controls the width of the form and also centers it. *Font*-styling for the form affects *only* the labels and legends. I wanted a larger font-size for the user inputs as well, so I had to create separate styling for them.

```
input[type="text"], input[type="email"], textarea {
  margin-bottom: .25em;
  padding: .25em;
  font-size: 1em;
}
```

As you can see, the syntax varies, depending on the type of inputs you're styling.

- For single-line text and email inputs, the selectors are **input[type="text"]** and **input[type="email"]**.

- For a textarea, it's just **textarea**.

I wanted a hefty Submit button, so I coded this styling.

```
input[type="submit"] {
  font-size: 1.25em;
}
```

The button will expand to accommodate the enlarged text.
I bolded the legends.

```
legend {
  font-weight: 700;
}
```

In your CSS file double the font-size of text input and textarca controls, and give them some padding all around. Save the file. Display the page. Sample CSS code is at http://asmarterwaytolearn.com/htmlcss/practice-58-1.html.

Find the interactive coding exercises for this chapter at:
http://www.ASmarterWayToLearn.com/htmlcss/58.html

59
COMMENTS

Commenting is a way to tell the browser to ignore certain portions of text that you include within the body of code. Comments are for the human, not the machine. They help you and others understand your code when it comes time to revise. You can also use commenting to *comment out* portions of your code for testing and debugging.

In HTML any text enclosed by an opening **<!--** tag and a closing **-->** tag is invisible to the browser. In the following code "Beginning of questionnaire form" is a comment that the browser ignores.

```
<!-- Beginning of questionnaire form -->
<form action="questionnaire.php" method="post">
  <fieldset>
    <legend>Contact info</legend>
    <label>First name: <input type="text" name="first-name"
size="15" maxlength="30"></label>
[etc.]
```

Here's a multi-line comment. When you write a multi-line comment, put the tags on their own separate lines for readability.

```
<!--
Note to myself. Think about combining the
questionnaire form with the feedback form.
-->
```

You can also comment CSS code, but the tags are different. It's **/*** to open, ***/** to close.

```
/* Styles for headings */
h1 {
  font-size: 3em;
}
h2 {
[etc.]
```

You can have mutli-line CSS comments. Again, put tags on their own separate lines for readability.

```
/*
This CSS file was created on May 28, 2018.
The styles are optimized for a learning site.
*/
```

In your HTML file add a multi-line comment. In your CSS file add a multi-line comment. Save the files. Display the page. (The HTML comment should not display.)

Sample HTML code is at http://asmarterwaytolearn.com/htmlcss/practice-59-1.html. Sample CSS code is at http://asmarterwaytolearn.com/htmlcss/practice-59-2.html.

Find the interactive coding exercises for this chapter at:
http://www.ASmarterWayToLearn.com/htmlcss/59.html

60
LAYOUT: NESTED BOXES

The first thing to know about HTML page layout is that it's always a collection of invisible nested boxes. Everything, from the header to the shortest paragraph or tiniest icon, is inside something else.

In an earlier chapter you learned that all of the content of a webpage is enclosed by an opening **\<body\>** tag and closing **\</body\>** tag. This means that the body is the biggest box, the box that contains everything else. (Well, it's the biggest box your CSS code can affect. The body is actually inside the box created by the opening **\<html\>** and closing **\</html\>** tags.) Think of the body as the brown box with the Amazon logo on it that the postal carrier delivers. All the other boxes are inside it. To take the metaphor even further, the outermost box, defined by the opening and closing **\<html\>** tags, which you never deal with except to write the tags, is the mail truck.

How many boxes are contained inside the big outer box (the body), and how many levels of nesting wind up inside it, are decisions you make, depending on what you want your page to look like. At a minimum, most professional websites include a collection of boxes that looks something like this.

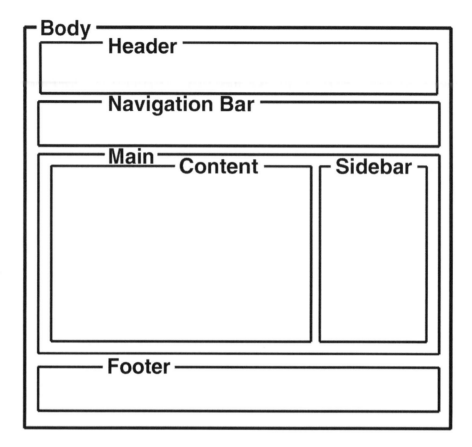

Of the boxes shown in the diagram, the only big box that you absolutely must have in your code is the outer box created by the required opening **<body>** and closing **</body>** tags. You can, if you choose, put all of your headings, paragraphs, images, and links inside that one big, undifferentiated box, and some people do. You've seen such pages. The text stretches all the way across the browser window. There's no layout, really. You exit the site as fast as you can.

The diagram above shows the boxes that represent major sections of the page. If I had wanted to show all the smaller boxes that are contained within those boxes, I would have included the boxes containing text. These boxes are created by opening **<p>** and closing **</p>** tags, opening and closing heading tags, opening **<ul>** and closing **</ul>** tags, and opening **<li>** and closing **</li>** tags. On an HTML page, everything is inside something else. Whenever you write an HTML tag, you create a box. The opening **<p>** and closing **</p>** tags in the following example create a box containing the text "Hey now!"

```
<p>Hey now!</p>
```

In the following example the opening **<a>** and closing **</a>** tags create a box containing the text "Stack Overflow."

```
<a href="http://www.stackoverflow.com">Stack Overflow</a>
```

For any box of any size, its contents are affected by any styles you specify for that box. So if you write…

```
p {
  color: purple;
}
```

…all the text enclosed by an opening **<p>** tag or a closing **</p>** tag will be, God help you, purple.

…*unless* you make an exception. For example, you can write…

```
.sane-color {
  color: black;
}
```

Then, although the general style for paragraphs is still purple, any text enclosed by a tag that begins **<p class="sane-color..."** will be black.

Or you could write…

```
<p>This is <span class="sane-color">not</span> a pretty sentence.</p>
```

…and you've created a **span** box within the paragraph box that colors the word "not" black, while the rest of the sentence is purple.

Here's some styling for the biggest box, the box that contains everything else, the body.

```
body {
  width: 100%;
  font-family: Georgia, "Times New Roman", Times, serif;
  font-size: 1em;
  background-color: white;
  color: black;
}
```

Since the body is the biggest box, this bit of CSS means that all the text on the page, including all paragraphs, headings, table text, and list items, will be black on a white background, will be in the Georgia font or a variant, and will be based on the browser's default text size.

...*unless* you make an exception. And of course, you might make all kinds of exceptions, on just about every level. For example, you can create a general style for paragraphs that differs from the default for all text established in the **body** style. Another example: when you explicitly call for purple text as a **p** style, all text enclosed in **<p>** tags is purple rather than the body's default black. As you learned in an earlier chapter, you can also make exceptions to *that* rule by creating classes and IDs for paragraphs that specify different characteristics.

Later I'll discuss the **width: 100%** and **font-size: 1em** specifications in the **body** style shown above. But first we need to talk about how to create the big sections, like the header and main sections, shown in the diagram above.

Find the interactive coding exercises for this chapter at:
http://www.ASmarterWayToLearn.com/htmlcss/60.html

61
LAYOUT: DIVS

All the boxes that constitute an HTML layout are contained in the big box created by the opening **\<body\>** and closing **\</body\>** tags—the tags that begin and end the main section of every HTML document. In the diagram in the last chapter, you saw some relatively large boxes nested inside the big outermost Body box. What the diagram doesn't show is all the smaller boxes nested inside these relatively large boxes. The smaller boxes are created by the opening and closing tags for headings, paragraphs, list items, and so on.

So how do you create the relatively large boxes, for the header, navigation section, main section, and so on—the boxes shown inside the big Body box in the diagram?

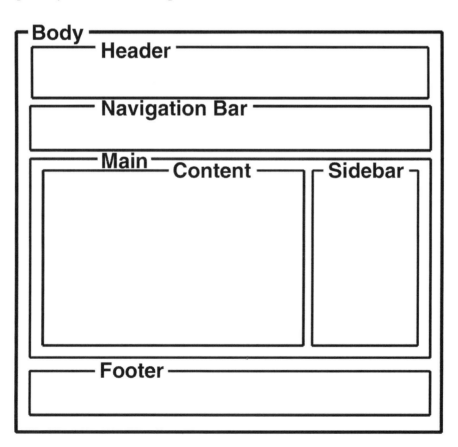

You create these boxes by using **div** tags. For example:

```
<div id="content">
  <h3>The slow loris.</h3>
  <img src="slow-loris.jpg" alt="Slow loris" width="55"
height="85">
  <p>Slow lorises are a group of several species of
primates which make up the genus Nycticebus.</p>
</div>
```

In the example, there are three elements grouped together inside the **div**—a heading, an image, and a paragraph. Just as any styling that you specify for the body will be applied to all elements contained in the body unless you make explicit exceptions, any styling that you specify for the **div** will be applied to all elements inside the **div** unless you make explicit exceptions. In the HTML code above, I've created a **div** with an id of "content." I'll style the **div** with a color.

```
div#content {
  color: red;
}
```

With this style, the heading and paragraph text in the **div** will be red—unless you create exceptions. An exception would be if you've explicitly specified a particular color for **h3** headings or a particular color for paragraphs. Then those specifications will override the default color that you're specifying for the **div**.

Styling precedence works like this:

- Styling for an inner box overrides styling for an outer box. For example, in the last chapter we specified black as the color for all the text in the body. Black is the color unless otherwise specified. This default is overridden by the **div** we created above, which calls for red text. So now the default color for all the text in the **div** is red.

- Styling for an element, like a paragraph, overrides styling for a **div**. This is really the same rule as the first rule above, since the box created by **<p>** tags is inside the box created by the **<div>** tags, and the rule says that styling for an inner box overrides styling for an outer box. Styling for the **div** says black, but we create a style for all **p** elements that says purple, the purple paragraph style will override the **div** black style.

- Class and id styling override general styling. If we create a "sane-color" class of paragraphs, the general purple specification for paragraphs is overridden for any paragraphs whose tag begins **<p class="sane-color..."**

Why did I create an id for the **div** rather than a class? Because this particular **div**—the one that contains all the content on the page— occurs just once in the document. A class can be used more than once, an id only once. If we were styling a **div** that might occur more than once in the HTML, we'd create a class rather than an id.

As you've seen in this chapter, a **div** is handy for setting default styling within a section, but the most important function of **div**s is layout positioning. That's next.

Find the interactive coding exercises for this chapter at:
http://www.ASmarterWayToLearn.com/htmlcss/61.html

62
LAYOUT: DIV WIDTHS AND CENTERING

Consider the **div** that contains most of the page's content, the one that, in our example, creates the Main box. It's the third box down in the diagram shown in the last chapter. We'll give the **div** an id of "main."

Usually, you don't want the contents of a section to bump up against the left and right edges of the window. As in a book, you create some whitespace on the left and right. A good way to do it is to specify a width for the section, like this.

```
div#main {
  width: 90%;
}
```

When you specify **em**s or percentages, these values are always relative to what's "normal"—either the browser's default or a style you've overridden with CSS styling. In our example, we created a default width in the body styling, **width: 100%**. This tells the browser to make the body width the full width of the browser window. That's the browser's default, so we're just telling it to do what it would do anyway. But by making it explicit, we tell any human readers trying to understand our CSS that we're accepting the browser's default.

So when you specify **width: 90%** for the main section, you're telling the browser to make the section only 90% as wide as the browser window. If we had specified **width: 60%** for the body, specifying **width: 90%** for the main section would make the section 60% times 90%, or 54% of the full window width.

Browsers place things on the left. This means that if we make the main section narrower than the body, the main section will bump up against the left edge of the browser window, and all the whitespace will be on the right. We want the section centered. So we add a line.

177

```
div#main {
  width: 90%;
  margin: 0 auto 0 auto;
}
```

Specifying **auto** for left and right margins tells the browser that if there's any width left over—in this case 10%—to split the difference. Now there'll be a margin on the left that's equal to 5% of the browser window width and a margin on the right of the same width. That is, the section will be centered.

You can make the section narrower, with wider margins, by reducing the percentage you specify for the width. You can add whitespace above and/or below the section by replacing the zeros with **em** values.

```
div#main {
  width: 90%;
  margin: 1.5em auto 1% auto;
}
```

Play around with the **em** values to get the margins to suit you.

Suppose you have several **div**s within the main **div**, and you want to give these proportionally the same margins that you've assigned to the main **div** (not that the margins *have* to be proportional). You could do this by using exactly the same specifications you used for the main **div**.

```
div.inset {
  width: 90%;
  margin 0 auto 0 auto;
}
```

Since all values of the inner **div** are relative to the values of the outer **div**, the **div**s of the class "inset" will have 90% of the width of the outer **div**. This is the result.

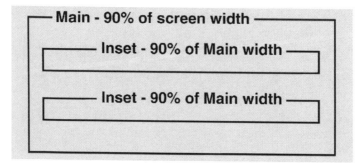

Of course, the inner **div**'s width value doesn't have to be the same as the width value of the outer **div**. I just did it this way so you can see that the width of the inner **div**, though it shares the same value, is narrower than the outer **div**, since it's 90% of 90% of the body width, whereas the outer **div** is 90% of the full body width.

In Chapter 60 I promised to discuss two specifications in the body styling:

```
body {
    width: 100%;
    font-family: Georgia, "Times New Roman", Times, serif;
    font-size: 1em;
    background-color: white;
    color: black;
}
```

A moment ago, I discussed the **width: 100%** specification for the body style, saying that it's redundant in the sense that you're telling the browser to do what it would do anyway. The purpose is to help other coders, by explicitly saying that you're accepting the default width—the full width of the browser window—as the body width that the styles that follow will be based on. The same applies to **font-size: 1em**. You're letting other coders know that you're accepting the browser's default size as the value that all other styles will be based on.

In your CSS file code a **div** id that's 20% wide and centered. In your HTML file code the div and put a paragraph in it. Save the files. Display the page.

Sample CSS code is at http://asmarterwaytolearn.com/htmlcss/practice-62-1.html. Sample HTML code is at http://asmarterwaytolearn.com/htmlcss/practice-62-2.html.

Find the interactive coding exercises for this chapter at:
http://www.ASmarterWayToLearn.com/htmlcss/62.html

63
LAYOUT: SIDE-BY-SIDE DIVS

Look at the box diagram again. I've made a small change to it. I've nudged the Content section left, so it's up against the left side of the Main box, and the Sidebar section right, so it's up against the right side of the Main box. In the original diagram, I left some space between these two sections and the Main section so you could see all the boxes clearly, but I don't really want any extra whitespace on the left and right between the outer box and the two inner boxes.

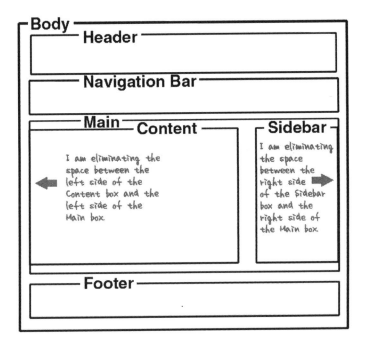

I want the two sections to sit side-by-side. I want no extra whitespace on the left or right, separating them from the outer Main box. This is how we do it.

First, we specify a width for each of the two inner boxes so when their widths are added together they don't add up to more than 100% of the width of the **div** that contains them, the Main box. But since I don't want them bumping up against each other in the middle, I'm going to give them widths that add up to just 97%. This leaves the remaining 3% for a center gutter between them. Here's the code.

```
div#content {
  width: 68%;
}
div#sidebar {
  width: 29%;
}
```

So far, this styling doesn't prevent the browser from placing one element underneath the other. If we don't do something about it, the second **div** will go right underneath the first **div**, since a **div** is a block element. Both of them will be flush with the left edge of the Main box. So we need to do one more thing. Remember how you learned to write **float: left** and **float: right** to style an image so text wraps around it? We use the same language to place the two **div**s side-by-side.

```
div#content {
  width: 68%;
  float: left;
}
div#sidebar {
  width: 29%;
  float: right;
}
```

Now they're side-by-side, and there's a gutter between them that's 3% of the width of their containing element, the Main box.

Let me give you another example. Suppose you want three **div**s of equal width placed side-by-side.

```
div#d1 {
  width: 31%;
  float: left;
}
div#d2 {
  width: 31%;
  float: left;
  margin: 0 0 0 3.5%;
}
div#d3 {
  width: 31%;
  float: right;
}
```

The first two **div**s are floated left. The third **div** is floated right. Each **div** is 31% wide, adding up to a total of 93% of the width of the containing Main box. That leaves 7% for the two gutters. I specify a left margin of 3.5% for the second **div**, forcing it to the right. This leaves 3.5% for the second gutter. Now the three sections are spaced evenly.

Remember learning in Chapter 27 that you need to clear image floats to avoid unintended wraps? You do the same thing with **div** floats.

```
.no-wrap {
  clear: both;
}
```

After coding side-by-side **div**s in HTML, you'd code an empty div whose only purpose is to clear the float above it.

```
<div class="no-wrap"></div>
```

Or you could do it with a paragraph that clears the float.

In your CSS file create two **div** ids that will place the divs side-by-side, with a gutter of whitespace between them. In your HTML file code the two divs and put a paragraph in each one. Save the files. Display the page.

Sample CSS code is at http://asmarterwaytolearn.com/htmlcss/practice-63-1.html. Sample HTML code is at http://asmarterwaytolearn.com/htmlcss/practice-63-2.html.

Find the interactive coding exercises for this chapter at:
http://www.ASmarterWayToLearn.com/htmlcss/63.html

64
LAYOUT: A MODERN HEADER PART 1

The box diagram we've been working with shows the header section scaled a little narrower than the body section, with some whitespace at the top.

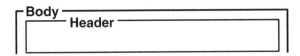

When the page displays, there's a small amount of whitespace between the top edge of the window and the top of the header. And there's a small amount of whitespace also on both sides of the header. This happens automatically if you don't override it.

A header with whitespace all around it is acceptable, but a more modern design would have the header on a color block that is flush with the top of the window and stretches all the way across the window from edge to edge. The box diagram would look like this.

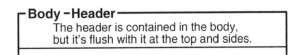

We start by making the header stretch from edge to edge. And we create the color block by giving it a background-color of dark crimson.

```
div#header {
  width: 100%
  background-color: #990000;
}
```

This is the HTML that creates the **div**.

```
<div id="header">
  [The contents of the div will go here.]

</div>
```

By specifying a width of 100%, we've asked the browser to stretch the **div** from edge-to-edge, but the browser isn't cooperating fully. It's still leaving a little whitespace on the left and right edges.

So we need to force the issue:

```
div#header {
  width: 100%
  position: absolute;
  left: 0;
  background-color: #990000;
}
```

By specifying **position: absolute**, we override whatever the browser *thinks* we mean by **width: 100%** and explicitly tell it where we want the left edge to start. By specifying **left: 0**, we say, "Start it 0 pixels in from the left edge of the window." In other words, eliminate all whitespace. Happily, without any additional instructions, the browser eliminates all whitespace on the right edge as well.

But, thanks to the browser's tendency to surround a **div** with whitespace, we still have a gap *above* the header. How do we solve this? You can probably guess.

```
div#header {
  width: 100%
  position: absolute;
  top: 0;
  left: 0;
  background-color: #990000;
}
```

Now we've told the browser to start the **div** 0 pixels from the top of the window. The gap disappears.

So do we see a color block at the top of the browser? No. If you open the page in a browser, the color block isn't anywhere to be found.

In the next chapter I'll deal with this.

Find the interactive coding exercises for this chapter at:
http://www.ASmarterWayToLearn.com/htmlcss/64.html

65
LAYOUT: A MODERN HEADER PART 2

In the last chapter we took the first steps to create a header that's flush with the top of the browser window and stretches from edge to edge of the window. We specified a width of 100% for the **div**. We instructed the browser to eliminate the whitespace it would normally add to the top and sides. And we added a background color.

But no header color block showed up. Why? Because without a height specification or any content that would force the browser to stretch the **div** up and down to accommodate the content, the browser assigns the **div** a height of 0. The crimson color block has a width but no height. It's one-dimensional, an invisible phantom.

We could assign it a height, specifying a number of pixels, but we're avoiding pixels because they prevent the page from adapting to different-size windows. We could assign it a height as a percentage to avoid the pixel problem, but we don't need to. When we put some content inside the **div**, the **div** will expand to accommodate it. For content, I'll start with a heading.

We start by creating a style for the heading.

```
div#header h2 {
   font-family: Verdana, Geneva, sans-serif;
   font-weight: 900;
   color: white;
}
```

The highlighted first line says, "Apply this style to an **h2** heading within the **div** whose id is "header."

Now we can write...

```
<div id="header">
   <h2>A Smarter Way to Learn</h2>
</div>
```

...and a header appears in the browser.

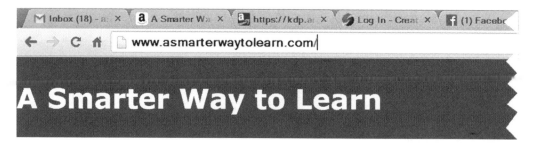

I'd like to make the heading a little beefier, so I add this:

```
div#header h2 {
    font-family: Verdana, Geneva, sans-serif;
    font-weight: 900;
    color: white;
    font-size: 2em;
}
```

This is the result:

Finally, let's give the heading some whitespace on the left.

```
div#header h2 {
    font-family: Verdana, Geneva, sans-serif;
    font-weight: 900;
    color: white;
    font-size: 2em;
    margin-left: 2%;
    padding: 0;
}
```

And here we go:

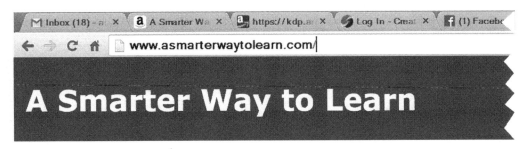

In your CSS file code a 100%-wide **div** with absolute positioning at the top left. Assign it a light color. In your HTML file code the **div** and put a heading in it. Save the files. Display the page. (The **div** will be at the top of the page if you coded correctly.)

Sample CSS code is at http://asmarterwaytolearn.com/htmlcss/practice-65-1.html. Sample HTML code is at http://asmarterwaytolearn.com/htmlcss/practice-65-2.html.

Find the interactive coding exercises for this chapter at:
http://www.ASmarterWayToLearn.com/htmlcss/65.html

66

LAYOUT: A MODERN HEADER PART 3

Let's add a logo to the header. We'll place it to the left of the header text. Here's a start:

```
<div id="header">
   <img src="images/logo_led_bulb.png" alt="logo" width="40"
height="47">
   <h2>A Smarter Way to Learn</h2>
</div>
```

That gives us this:

That's not what we want. We'll have to float the image.

```
div#header img {
   float: left;
}
```

Here's what the float accomplishes:

We're getting close. We just need to add some space around the logo.

```
div#header img {
  float: left;
  margin: .9em .6em 0 .75em;
}
```

And there you have it.

Notice that the color block—the **div**—has expanded vertically to accommodate the top and bottom margins.

1. In your CSS file style the image inside the **div** so it floats left and has **1em** of margin.

2. Give the heading inside the div some top-padding so it moves down to center vertically.

3. In your HTML file add an image inside the **div**: http://www.asmarterwaytolearn.com/loris_50.jpg

4. Save the file and display the page. (Don't be surprised to see the header cover up some content. We'll deal with this in Chapter 68.)

Sample CSS code is at http://asmarterwaytolearn.com/htmlcss/practice-66-1.html. Sample HTML code is at http://asmarterwaytolearn.com/htmlcss/practice-66-2.html.

Find the interactive coding exercises for this chapter at:
http://www.ASmarterWayToLearn.com/htmlcss/66.html

67
LAYOUT: A MODERN HEADER PART 4

In the last chapter you learned how to force the browser to position a **div** precisely where you want it. The header that we created using this approach appears in that position when the page first displays. Then if the user scrolls the page, the header scrolls with all the other content. But you can tell a browser to *leave* a div where you put it, to *not* scroll it when the page scrolls. For example, you might want the header to stay visible at the top of the browser window as everything below it scrolls. Here's the code. (I'm omitting all the header styling that I covered in the last chapter.)

```
div#header {
  position: fixed;
  top: 0;
  left: 0;
}
```

position: fixed tells the browser to keep the **div** immobilized as everything else on the page scrolls. This makes the **div**'s position within the window permanent. As you learned in the last chapter, **top: 0** and **left: 0** tell the browser to place the header flush against the top of the window and flush against the left side of the window.

If you were to write this…

```
div#ad-box {
  postion: fixed;
  top: 150px;
  left: 50px;
}
```

…the **div** with the id "ad-box" would be permanently positioned 150 pixels from the top of the window and 50 pixels in from the left side of the window.

You can also specify a position some distance (or no distance) in from the right side of the window. The following code positions the ad box flush against the top of the window and 10 pixels in from the right.

193

```
div#ad-box {
  postion: fixed;
  top: 0;
  right: 10px;
}
```

Alternatively, you can specify a position some distance (or no distance) up from the bottom of the window.

```
div#footer {
  position: fixed;
  bottom: 0;
  left: 0;
}
```

I've coded the positions in pixels, because that's easier for you to understand. But, as you know, percentages are preferable, so…

```
div#ad-box {
  postion: fixed;
  top: 0;
  right: 2%;
}
```

In your CSS file change the absolutely-positioned div to fixed position. Save the file and display the page. Try scrolling down from the top. (Don't be surprised to see the header cover up some content. We'll deal with this in the next chapter.)

Sample CSS code is at http://asmarterwaytolearn.com/htmlcss/practice-67-1.html.

Find the interactive coding exercises for this chapter at:
http://www.ASmarterWayToLearn.com/htmlcss/67.html

In the last two chapters we created headers with a fixed position at the top of the browser window. In Chapter 66, you learned to create a header with *absolute* positioning that scrolls. In Chapter 67, you learned to create a header with *fixed* positioning that doesn't scroll. We'll soon be adding more to the HTML document, with the intention of building a page whose content looks like this. (I'm showing only a top portion of the page.)

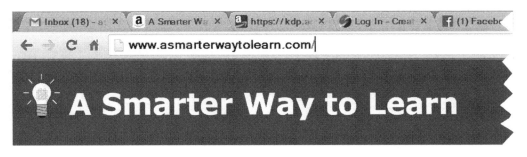

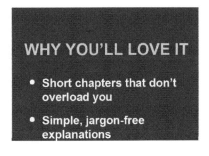

The picture above shows what we want, but that's not what we're going to get. When you specify **position: absolute** or **position: fixed**, you remove the **div** from the normal flow of the HTML page. The **div** goes where you tell it to go, ignoring the natural flow of the other HTML elements. They return the favor by totally ignoring the **div** element. They behave as if it weren't there. What this means is that when you force a header to take a particular position, the other stuff on the page won't respectfully make room for it. Since the other elements don't know it's there, they'll position themselves as if it *isn't* there, right where the **div** is, violating the natural law that says two things can't occupy the same space. Unaware of the **div**, they'll flow normally and will wind up *under* the div. They'll be invisible

You *could* style the sidebar and main section with big top margins to move them down below the header so they're in the clear. But I prefer a more elegant solution.

Create a *duplicate* of the header—a copy of it that isn't fixed, a header that is part of the main flow. You make this header visible to the browser but invisible to the user. In effect, it's a spacer.

```
div#invisible-header {
    width: 100%;
    visibility: hidden;
}
```

Add a new selector to the header's **h2** styling so the invisible heading is styled like the visible heading:

```
div#header h2, div#invisible-header h2 {
    font-family: Verdana, Geneva, sans-serif;
    font-weight: 900;
    color: white;
    font-size: 2em;
    margin-left: 2%;
    padding: 0;
}
```

Do the same thing for the image.

```
div#header img, div#invisible-header img {
    float: left;
    margin: .9em .6em 0 .75em;
}
```

visibility: hidden, specified for the header **div** and everything it encloses, tells the browser to keep its contents invisible (though the browser knows it's there).

Since we floated the image, we need a paragraph that clears the float. We'll style it this way:

```
p.clearFloat {
   clear: both;
}
```

The HMTL code for the invisible header and its contents is inserted at the top of the page.

```
<body>
<div id="invisible-header">
   <img src="robot-logo-bust.png" alt="logo">
   <h2>A Smarter Way to Learn</h2>
</div>
```

For precision placement of the elements immediately below the header, you may need to adjust the margin of the spacer **div**. Since the browser will add a little whitespace above the spacer **div**, it's going to drop a little below the visible header. To move it up so it mimics the visible header, give it some negative top-margin.

Why is the visible fixed header covering up the other elements instead of the other way around? Because by default a fixed-position element goes on top. But you can interfere with this *stack order*, using **z-index**. The lower the **z-index** number, the lower its place in the stack order. All elements that are in the normal HTML flow have an implicit **z-index** of 0.

In your CSS file, code invisible versions of the fixed-position **div**, its heading, and its image. In your HTML file insert the **div** and its contents at the top of the page contents, under **<body>**.

Sample CSS code is at http://asmarterwaytolearn.com/htmlcss/practice-68-1.html. Sample HTML code is at http://asmarterwaytolearn.com/htmlcss/practice-68-2.html.

Find the interactive coding exercises for this chapter at:
http://www.ASmarterWayToLearn.com/htmlcss/68.html

69
A VERTICAL NAVIGATION BAR PART 1

Since a navigation bar presents the user with a list of choices, the usual way to make one is to code an unordered list. Here's some code.

```
<div id="navbar">
  <ul>
    <li>Why Choose Us</li>
    <li>Recent Projects</li>
    <li>Our Team</li>
    <li>Get a Quote</li>
    <li>Contact Us</li>
  </ul>
</div>
```

This is what it looks like so far.

- Why Choose Us
- Recent Projects
- Our Team
- Get a Quote
- Contact Us

It isn't a navigation bar if it isn't clickable. So let's add some links.

```
<div id="navbar">
  <ul>
    <li><a href="why-choose-us.html">Why Choose Us</a></li>
    <li><a href="recent-projects.html">Recent
Projects</a></li>
    <li><a href="our-team.html">Our Team</a></li>
    <li><a href="get-a-quote.html">Get a Quote</a></li>
    <li><a href="contact-us.html">Contact Us</a></li>
  </ul>
</div>
```

- <u>Why Choose Us</u>
- <u>Recent Projects</u>
- <u>Our Team</u>
- <u>Get a Quote</u>
- <u>Contact Us</u>

Now the list items are blue and are underlined, indicating links.

Since it's going to be a navigation bar, we don't need the bullets. This is the code that removes them.

```
div#navbar ul {
  list-style-type: none;
}
```

Now the bullets are gone.

<u>Why Choose Us</u>
<u>Recent Projects</u>
<u>Our Team</u>
<u>Get a Quote</u>
<u>Contact Us</u>

We'll continue with the navigation bar in the next chapter.

1. In your CSS file, code a **div** id for a navigation bar. Include an id. Give it a **clear: both** specification to prevent wrap from the **div** above it.

2. Style an unordered list within the **div** so it has no bullets.

3. In your HTML file, code the **div**.

4. Within the **div**, code an unordered list with links. Make up the links. They don't have to work.

5. Save the files. Display the page.

Sample CSS code is at http://asmarterwaytolearn.com/htmlcss/practice-69-1.html. Sample HTML code is at http://asmarterwaytolearn.com/htmlcss/practice-69-2.html.

Find the interactive coding exercises for this chapter at:
http://www.ASmarterWayToLearn.com/htmlcss/69.html

70
A VERTICAL NAVIGATION BAR PART 2

In the last chapter, we started constructing a navigation bar. We created an unordered list, made the list items clickable, and removed the bullets. Now let's style the anchors. The style will apply to all anchors that are list items in an unordered list in the **div** with an id of "navbar."

```
div#navbar ul li a {
    font-family: Arial, Helvetica, sans-serif;
    font-size: 1.1em;
    font-weight: 900;
}
```

Now we have this.

Why Choose Us

Recent Projects

Our Team

Get a Quote

Contact Us

Since it's a navigation bar, we can assume that the user knows it's clickable. We don't need the underline to communicate that the text items are links. So…

```
div#navbar ul li a {
    font-family: Arial, Helvetica, sans-serif;
    font-size: 1.1em;
    font-weight: 900;
    text-decoration: none;
}
```

This is the result.

Why Choose Us
Recent Projects
Our Team
Get a Quote
Contact Us

We'll continue constructing the navigation bar in the next chapter.
In your CSS file, make the anchors bigger, bolder, and sans-serif.
Take away the underlines. Save the file. Display the page.
Sample CSS code is at
http://asmarterwaytolearn.com/htmlcss/practice-70-1.html.

Find the interactive coding exercises for this chapter at:
http://www.ASmarterWayToLearn.com/htmlcss/70.html

71
A VERTICAL NAVIGATION BAR PART 3

In the last chapter we styled the anchors. Now let's give the **div** a blue background.

```
div#navbar {
  background-color: blue;
}
```

We'll make the anchors white so they show up on the blue background.

```
div#navbar ul li a {
  font-family: Arial, Helvetica, sans-serif;
  font-size: 1.1em;
  font-weight: 900;
  text-decoration: none;
  color: white;
}
```

And we'll style the **div** so it's just wide enough to accommodate the list items, but no wider.

```
div#navbar {
  clear: both;
  background-color: blue;
  display: inline-block;
}
```

inline-block tells the browser to shrink to fit.

Now we have…

The browser hasn't forgotten that this is a list, so it has added padding on the left side to indent it. We don't want it indented. So we specify zero left-side padding for the **ul**.

```
div#navbar ul {
    list-style-type: none;
    padding-left: 0;
}
```

That moves it flush-left.

Because an unordered list is a block element, the browser has added top and bottom margins. We'll keep them.

In your CSS file…

1. Make the navigation bar **div** a dark color.

2. Make the anchors a light color.

3. Shrink the navigation bar to fit.

4. Remove padding from the left side of the list.

5. Save the file. Display the page.

Sample CSS code is at
http://asmarterwaytolearn.com/htmlcss/practice-71-1.html.

Find the interactive coding exercises for this chapter at:
http://www.ASmarterWayToLearn.com/htmlcss/71.html

72
A VERTICAL NAVIGATION BAR PART 4

We're still working on the vertical navigation bar. Here's what we have so far.

I want the color block to expand horizontally. We could do this by adding left and right padding to the **ul**, but because of something we're going to do in the next chapter, I'll add the padding to the **li** elements instead.

```
div#navbar ul li {
  padding: 0 1em 0 1em;
}
```

This is the result.

Now we'll add a little padding below each list item to separate them.

```
div#navbar ul li {
    padding: 0 1em .3em 1em;
}
```

The result:

In your CSS file, add some padding on the left and right of list items. Add a little padding to the bottom of each list item to separate them. Save the file. Display the page.

Sample CSS code is at http://asmarterwaytolearn.com/htmlcss/practice-72-1.html.

Find the interactive coding exercises for this chapter at:
http://www.ASmarterWayToLearn.com/htmlcss/72.html

73
A VERTICAL NAVIGATION BAR PART 5

The vertical navigation bar we created in the last chapter is functional, but doesn't look that great. Let's dress it up a little.

Instead of a list of links against a blue background, we're going to have five separate blue blocks. Each block is a navigation choice.

We remove the blue background from the **div**, since we're going to color the **li** elements individually.

```
div#navbar {
  background-color: blue;
  display:inline-block;
  clear: both;
}
```

The styling for the unordered list is unchanged…

```
div#navbar ul {
  list-style-type: none;
  padding-left: 0;
}
```

We're going to color each **li** element separately, so we write…

```
div#navbar ul li {
  background-color: blue;
  padding: 0 1em .3em 1em;
}
```

We're going to stretch out the blue **li** elements by padding the **a** elements inside them, so we no longer need padding on the **li** elements.

```
div#navbar ul li {
  background-color: blue;
  padding: 0 1em .3em 1em;
}
```

To enlarge the blue background of the **li** elements, we declare each **a** element a block and pad it out.

```
div#navbar ul li a {
   font-family: Arial, Helvetica, sans-serif;
   font-size: 3em;
   font-weight: 900;
   text-decoration: none;
   color: white;
   display: block;
   padding: .35em;
  }
```

All these changes produce this.

Separate the list items with a little bit of bottom margin…

```
div#navbar ul li {
   background-color: blue;
   margin: 0 0 .25em 0;
}
```

And there you have it:

Revise your CSS file to style the navbar like the one shown above. Save the file. Display the page. (Code the **li** bottom margin as above, specifying 0 for the other three sides, to override a general margin specification for **li** elements that you coded earlier.)

Sample CSS code is at
http://asmarterwaytolearn.com/htmlcss/practice-73-1.html.

Find the interactive coding exercises for this chapter at:
http://www.ASmarterWayToLearn.com/htmlcss/73.html

74
A HORIZONTAL NAVIGATION BAR PART 1

You don't need to know much more than you already know in order to create a horizontal navigation bar. Like a vertical navigation bar, it's just a list of links with some styling.

We'll start by replacing the shrink-to-fit **inline-block** specification with a width.

```
div#navbar {
  display:inline-block;
  width: 100%;
}
```

The **ul** styling is the same as before.

```
div#navbar ul {
  list-style-type: none;
}
```

The **a** element styling has only one change.

```
div#navbar ul li a {
  font-family: Arial, Helvetica, sans-serif;
  font-size: 1.1em;
  font-weight: 900;
  text-decoration: none;
  color: white;
  display: block;
  padding: .75em;
}
```

The big changes are in the **li** styling.

```
div#navbar ul li {
  background-color: blue;
  text-align: center;
  display: inline;
  width: 19%;
  float: left;
  margin-right: .5em;
}
```

display: inline tells the browser not to arrange the list items vertically, the default, but to put them side-by-side.

We want each of the five blocks to be the same width. By specifying that each block occupy 19% of the width of the **div**, we leave room for the margin that creates a little whitespace between each block.

float: left—well, you know how that works. It arrays the blocks horizontally across the window.

The **.5em** right margin separates the blocks with a little white space. We wouldn't have to do this, of course. We could skip the margin and have the navigation bar be a solid blue block across the window.

This is the result. (I'm showing you just the left half of the menu.)

Change your CSS file to convert the vertical menu to a horizontal menu. Save the file. Display the page.

Sample CSS code is at http://asmarterwaytolearn.com/htmlcss/practice-74-1.html.

Find the interactive coding exercises for this chapter at:
http://www.ASmarterWayToLearn.com/htmlcss/74.html

75
A HORIZONTAL NAVIGATION BAR PART 2

Let's add two more features to the navigation bar.

When the user hovers over a selection, the blue color block turns light blue.

In order to do this, we need to create special class for the **li** elements.

We start by removing a line we've already coded.

```
div#navbar ul li {
  background-color: blue;
  text-align: center;
  display: inline;
  width: 19%;
  float: left;
  margin-right: .5em;
}
```

Then we create the special **li** class.

```
li.changeBackground {
```

We start by coding a normal color for the class.

```
li.changeBackground {
  background-color: blue;
}
```

Then we code the hover state.

```
li.changeBackground:hover {
  background-color: lightBlue;
}
```

We can also code a color for the active state.

217

```
li.changeBackground:active {
  background-color: darkBlue;
}
```

When the user clicks a selection, the color block turns dark blue.

| Why Choose Us | Recent Projects | Our T |

This is the HTML.

```
<div id="navbar">
  <ul>
    <li class="changeBackground"><a href="why-choose-
us.html">Why Choose Us</a></li>
    <li class="changeBackground"><a href="recent-
projects.html">Recent Projects</a></li>
    <li class="changeBackground"> a href="our-
team.html">Our Team</a></li>
    <li class="changeBackground"><a href="get-a-
quote.html">Get a Quote</a></li>
    <li class="changeBackground"><a href="contact-
us.html">Contact Us</a></li>
  </ul>
</div>
```

Change your CSS and HTML files to create a class of list item that is one color to start with, a second color when it's moused over, and a third color when it's active. Save the files. Display the page.

Sample CSS code is at http://asmarterwaytolearn.com/htmlcss/practice-75-1.html. Sample HTML code is at http://asmarterwaytolearn.com/htmlcss/practice-75-2.html.

Find the interactive coding exercises for this chapter at:
http://www.ASmarterWayToLearn.com/htmlcss/75.html

76
BACKGROUND IMAGES PART 1

In previous chapters you learned how to underlay an element with a solid color using **background-color**. You can also underlay an element with an image. This is an example.

```
div#main {
  background-image: url("images/field-of-poppies.jgp");
}
```

The **div** with an id of "main" will be underlaid with the image whose URL is shown inside the parentheses and quotation marks.

You can put a background image behind any element. It's common to underlay the whole page with an image.

```
body {
  background-image: url("images/gray-gradient.png");
}
```

The entire page will be underlaid with the image whose URL is "images/gray-gradient.png".

In the example above, the image, which must be sized to fit the whole page, will be a large one, and so will take some time to load. If your background image is nothing but a repeating pattern, you can make it load faster by specifying a small slice for the image and asking the browser to repeat it.

You can cut this image down to a 1-pixel-wide slice that has the same height, and write this CSS:

```
body {
  background-image: url("images/gray-gradient-slice.png");
  background-repeat: repeat-x;
}
```

The slice will be tiled all across the width of the page (the x-axis), creating the same effect as the big image, but using a fast-loading small image.

Suppose you have a gradient fading from left-to-right rather than top-to-bottom. Then you would take a 1-pixel-high horizontal slice and tile it from top to bottom (the y-axis).

```
body {
  background-image: url("images/gray-gradient-slice.png");
  background-repeat: repeat-y;
}
```

If you have a background image that you want to repeat both horizonally and vertically, omit the **background-repeat:** specification.

```
body {
  background-image: url("images/gray-gradient-slice.png");
  background-repeat: repeat-x;
}
```

The browser will automatically tile the image in both directions to fill the page.

In your CSS file, find the **div** that's 20% wide. Tile the following image across the width of the div: http://www.asmarterwaytolearn.com/gray-gradient-slice.png. Save the file. Display the page. Check out the div.

Sample CSS code is at http://asmarterwaytolearn.com/htmlcss/practice-76-1.html.

Find the interactive coding exercises for this chapter at:
http://www.ASmarterWayToLearn.com/htmlcss/76.html

77
BACKGROUND IMAGES PART 2

Suppose you have an image that's smaller than the page and you want to keep it that way. You don't want it to repeat. But if you write…

```
body {
  background-image: url("images/faded-logo.png");
}
```

…the browser will automatically repeat it, to fill the page. So you write…

```
body {
  background-image: url("images/faded-logo.png");
  background-repeat: no-repeat;
}
```

A small image that doesn't repeat is placed, by default, at the left-upper corner. But you can specify a position.

```
body {
  background-image: url("images/faded-logo.png");
  background-repeat: no-repeat;
  background-position: right top;
}
```

Now the image will be positioned at the right-top corner.

The horizontal specifications are **left**, **center**, and **right**. The vertical specifications are **top**, **center**, and **bottom**. You always write the horizontal specification first. It's **left bottom**, never **bottom left**. If you want to center an image both horizontally and vertically, you write:

```
background-position: center;
```

Do you want the image to scroll with everything else? If so, you write…

```
body {
  background-image: url("images/faded-logo.png");
  background-repeat: no-repeat;
  background-position: right top;
  background-attachment: scroll;
}
```

If you want the image to stay put, you write…

```
body {
  background-image: url("images/faded-logo.png");
  background-repeat: no-repeat;
  background-position: right top;
  background-attachment: fixed;
}
```

In your CSS file, add a background image to the right top of the window. Don't let it repeat. Fix it in place. The image is http://www.asmarterwaytolearn.com/monarch.jpg. In your HTML file, use <!-- and --> to hide the fixed-position header from the browser so it doesn't display. Save the file. Display the page.

Sample CSS code is at http://asmarterwaytolearn.com/htmlcss/practice-77-1.html. Sample HTML code is at http://asmarterwaytolearn.com/htmlcss/practice-77-2.html.

Find the interactive coding exercises for this chapter at:
http://www.ASmarterWayToLearn.com/htmlcss/77.html

78
IFRAMES

An *iframe* is like your TV's picture-in-picture. It's an HTML page within an HTML page. For example, suppose I want to run the Metropolitan Opera's page inside my page. This is the HTML.

```
<iframe src="http://metopera.org/" width="700"
height="450"></iframe>
<p>The Metropolitan Opera, commonly referred to as the
"Met", is a company based in New York City, resident at the
Metropolitan Opera House at the Lincoln Center for the
Performing Arts. The company is operated by the non-profit
Metropolitan Opera Association, with Peter Gelb as etc.
```

Things to notice:

- There's an opening **<iframe>** tag and a closing **</iframe>** tag.

- **src="[URL]"** specifies the location of the HTML file that's to be imbedded, the same way **src="[URL]"** specifies the location of an image file. I've shortened the URL so you can focus on the syntax.

- You specify width and height in pixels. Scrollbars allow the user to explore the whole embedded page.

You can wrap text around an iframe.
This is the CSS.

```
iframe {
  float: left;
  margin: 0 2em 0 0;
}
```

In your HTML, create an **iframe** that embeds an online webpage of your choice. Save the file. Display the page. Adjust the dimensions of the **iframe** until you're happy with the result.

Sample HTML code is at
http://asmarterwaytolearn.com/htmlcss/practice-78-1.html.

Find the interactive coding exercises for this chapter at:
http://www.ASmarterWayToLearn.com/htmlcss/78.html

79
EMBEDDING YOUTUBE VIDEOS

There are several ways you can add video to your website. The easiest is to embed a YouTube or Vimeo video. Plus, when you let YouTube or Vimeo host the video free instead of storing it on your webhost's server, you avoid possible extra charges your webhost might hit you with for using extra bandwidth (video is a bandwidth hog).

For complete control, you can host videos yourself. The vast majority of site owners don't do it, though, because it's a headache. Because makers of devices, operating systems, and browsers can't agree on one video standard, you have to create a variety of different video files if you want your video to be seen by everybody. You're a shoe manufacturer who has to make sixteen different sizes.

Since it's *so* much easier to let YouTube or Vimeo handle the compatibility issues, that's what I'm going to focus on.

In the last chapter you learned how to place an exterior page inside an HTML page by coding an `iframe`. That's the method you use to embed a YouTube or Vimeo video.

Let's start with YouTube.

You can find out how to post a YouTube video at YouTube or elsewhere online. I'm going to assume you've produced your video and posted it to YouTube. Here's how to put it on your webpage.

1. Find your video on YouTube. Locate "Share" under the video window and click it.

2. Click "Embed."

3. Click "SHOW MORE."

4. Scroll down to see some choices you can make.

5. Click the Video size dropdown, and you can choose from four standard video sizes. You can also choose "Custom."

    If you choose a custom size, be sure to keep the ratio of width to height at 16 to 9. Otherwise, the picture will distort. To remember the ratio, picture a young person in the U.S. getting her driver's license (16 years old), and driving the number 9 around.

You can also use a ratio of 4 to 3. If you do, you'll need to change the Aspect Ratio on your video's Player controls panel. See the next chapter for more on this.

6. Next, look at the other choices you have, below the Video size dropdown.

You'll want to uncheck "Show suggested videos when the video finishes," unless you want the user to choose from a gallery of more YouTube videos when your video finishes.

"Enable privacy-enhanced mode" means that YouTube won't store information about visitors to your site unless they play the video. In most cases, you won't care about this.

7. When you've finished making your selections, copy and paste the YouTube-generated iframe code into your HTML document.

8. If you'd like to add a frame border, change the "0" to a "1".

```
<iframe width="640" height="360"
src="//www.youtube.com/embed/_tky2rAxBIU?rel=0"
frameborder="1" allowfullscreen></iframe>
```

9. If you don't want the user to be able to enlarge the frame to fullscreen size, delete **allowfullscreen**.

```
<iframe width="640" height="360"
src="//www.youtube.com/embed/_tky2rAxBIU?rel=0"
frameborder="1" allowfullscreen></iframe>
```

In your HTML file, replace the **iframe** you coded for the last chapter with an embedded YouTube video. It doesn't have to be your own video. Use mine if you like:
https://www.youtube.com/watch?v=_tky2rAxBIU

Save the file. Display the page and play the video. Sample HTML code is at http://asmarterwaytolearn.com/htmlcss/practice-79-1.html. Find the interactive coding exercises for this chapter at http://www.ASmarterWayToLearn.com/htmlcss/79.html

80
FURTHER CUSTOMIZING YOUTUBE VIDEOS

When you're embedding a video on your site, you may not want a YouTube video to *look* like a YouTube video.

When you banish the YouTube branding and controls, a YouTube logo will appear in the lower right corner before playback and when the user mouses over the video, but otherwise, you've got a video that looks proprietary.

You can choose from a number of options to make the video look and perform the way you want it to. But you have to go to Google, the owner of YouTube, to do it.

Begin by copying your video's YouTube ID from the YouTube URL for your video. It's the code that follows the equal sign.

Alternatively, you can copy the ID from the **iframe** code that YouTube originally generated for you.

```
<iframe width="640" height="360"
src="//www.youtube.com/embed/_tky2rAxBIU?rel=0"
frameborder="1" allowfullscreen></iframe>
```

Note that the ID ends at the last character before the question mark.

1. Go to https://developers.google.com/youtube/youtube_player_demo.

2. Paste your video's ID into the video ID field.

3. Click "Update player with selected options. Google replaces the demo videos with your video when you click "Update player with selected options." If your ID is correct, the four video thumbnails are replaced by your video. It plays. You can pause it while you choose custom options.

4. Next, click the **Show player parameters** button at the top of the panel. Another panel with an array of customizing choices displays.

5. Click **modestbranding** to banish the YouTube logo.

6. When you've finished making selections, once again click "Update Player with Selected Options" at the top of the panel.

7. The **iframe** embed code changes to reflect your selections. Copy and paste it into your HTML document.

In your HTML file, change your embedded video so it has modest branding. Save the file. Display the page.

Sample HTML code is at
http://asmarterwaytolearn.com/htmlcss/practice-80-1.html.

Find the interactive coding exercises for this chapter at:
http://www.ASmarterWayToLearn.com/htmlcss/80.html

81
EMBEDDING VIMEO VIDEOS

If YouTube is the network TV of online video, Vimeo is cable. It's a little classier, looks a little better, and is preferred by many creative people. It's free for the basic service. You can remove all Vimeo branding if you're willing to pay $199 a year.

The process of embedding a Vimeo video is similar to YouTube's.

I'm assuming you've produced your video and posted it to Vimeo. Here's how to put it on your webpage.

1. On your Videos page at Vimeo locate the video you want to embed. Click the paper-airplane icon at the upper right.
2. A new window opens. If you don't choose to customize, copy the **iframe** code and paste it into your HTML document, and you're done.
3. To customize, click **+ Show Options**.
4. Select the options to change from the dropdown.
5. Here you can specify the dimensions of the video player. Change the width or the height. Vimeo will automatically change the other dimension to preserve the ratio of 16 to 9.
6. By clicking on a color block or specifying a color by hex code you can change the color the video title. The color of the progress bar will change to match.
7. For a clean look, you'll probably want to uncheck **Portrait**, **Title**, **Byline**, and **Show text link underneath this video**.
8. To make the video play automatically, check **Autoplay this video**. To make it loop check **Loop this video**. Chances are, you don't want a video description. If you don't, leave the last item unchecked.
9. Copy the embed code and paste it into your HTML document.

For $59.95 a year Vimeo gives you additional customization options and other privileges including faster conversion. For $199 a year, the Vimeo logo goes away; you can, if you wish, insert your own logo.

In your HTML file, replace the embedded YouTube video with an embedded Vimeo video. Use mine if you like:

https://vimeo.com/97326700

Since you're running the HTML locally rather than on the Web, you need to insert **http:** at the beginning of the video URL so your page can connect to the video online. Save the file. Display the page.

Sample HTML code is at http://asmarterwaytolearn.com/htmlcss/practice-81-1.html.

Find the interactive coding exercises for this chapter at:
http://www.ASmarterWayToLearn.com/htmlcss/81.html

It's far easier to host your own audio files than your own video files, because the compatibility issues are tamer. If you use Audacity or another audio editor to save your file in just two formats, *mp3* and *Ogg Vorbis*, your audio will play in any modern browser, using HTML5. This is the code.

```
<audio controls>
  <source src="whatever.ogg">
  <source src="whatever.mp3">
</audio>
```

If a particular browser can't handle the Ogg Vorbis file, it'll play the mp3 file.

The **audio** tag shown above includes the optional **controls**. This tells the browser to make the player visible and allow the user to control it.

```
<audio controls>
  <source src="whatever.ogg">
  <source src="whatever.mp3">
</audio>
```

An alternative is to have the audio autoplay, with or without controls. The following code starts the audio automatically, without a visible player.

```
<audio autoplay>
  <source src="whatever.ogg">
  <source src="whatever.mp3">
</audio>
```

The following code starts the audio automatically *and* displays controls.

```
<audio controls autoplay>
  <source src="whatever.ogg">
  <source src="whatever.mp3">
</audio>
```

Be careful with autoplay. In most situations, users find it annoying.

You can add a paragraph inside the **audio** tags that displays if the user has an antique browser that doesn't handle HTML5.

```
<audio controls>
  <source src="whatever.ogg">
  <source src="whatever.mp3">
  <p>This browser doesn't support our audio format.</p>
</audio>
```

In your HTML file, insert a **
** at the bottom, then embed the audio files

http://www.asmarterwaytolearn.com/boing.ogg and

http://www.asmarterwaytolearn.com/boing.mp3. Save the file. Display the page. Play the audio.

Sample HTML code is at

http://asmarterwaytolearn.com/htmlcss/practice-82-1.html.

Find the interactive coding exercises for this chapter at:

http://www.ASmarterWayToLearn.com/htmlcss/82.html

83
EMS VS. PERCENTAGES VS. PIXELS

Ems, percentages, and pixels are three different units of measurement that you use to style the elements of a webpage. They're somewhat interchangeable. That is, although I've taught you, for example, to express **font-size** in **em**s, you can, if you like, express it in pixels or as a percentage.

Pixels are easy to work with, because they're simple and absolute. With pixels, you don't have to deal with the sometimes confusing relativism of **em**s and percentages. But the problem with pixels is that they *are* absolute. A CSS file full of pixel specifications doesn't adapt to different-size screens, because it *isn't* relative. The need for responsive design forces us to limit our use of pixels and stick mostly to **em**s and percentages. Here are the rules of thumb that many developers follow, and that I usually follow in this book.

- **Ems** — Use them for typography, margins, and padding.

- **Percentages** — Use them for **div**s, tables, iframes, and sometimes margins and padding.

- **Pixels** — Use them for images, borders, windows, iframes, and fixed, absolute, and relative positioning (see next chapter).

In your CSS file, style a new **div** class. Make it less than the full width of the window. Then style a new paragraph class. Make it less than the full width of the **div** and center it. In your HTML file, code a **div** of that class and, within it, a paragraph of that class. Save the files. Display the page.

Sample CSS code is at http://asmarterwaytolearn.com/htmlcss/practice-83-1.html. Sample HTML code is at http://asmarterwaytolearn.com/htmlcss/practice-83-2.html.

Find the interactive coding exercises for this chapter at:
http://www.ASmarterWayToLearn.com/htmlcss/83.html

84
RELATIVE AND STATIC POSITIONING

As you know, the browser displays the elements of your page in the same order in which you write them in your HTML document. If you write a heading, follow it with a paragraph, follow that with a table, and follow the table with a second paragraph, the browser will display everything in that order:

> Heading
> Paragraph 1
> Table
> Paragraph 2

But as you saw in Chapters 64 and 67, you can interfere with this natural order. In those chapters, you learned how to position a header exactly where you want it regardless of its order in the HTML document using absolute and fixed positioning.

So, with absolute and fixed positioning, where you place the code in the document doesn't affect its position on the page. You could add the code to the very end of the body section, put it somewhere in the middle, or start it off at the beginning. Its location on the page is determined by the position you specify in your CSS, not its position in the HTML document.

And remember, with these types of positioning, all the other elements behave as if they don't know the element is there. They don't make room for it, as they do for normally positioned elements. This creates overlap unless you pull a trick like the one you learned in Chapter 68, creating an invisible copy of the header that's positioned normally and so acts as a spacer, to keep the other normally-positioned elements from disappearing underneath the fixed-position header.

Both absolute and fixed positioning specify spacing in terms of how far they are from the edges of the browser window.

A third way to interfere with the browser's default layout is to specify *relative* positioning. Relative positioning tells the browser to position an element a certain distance from its normal position.

For example, if you wanted to position some paragraphs 50 pixels below their normal position, you could write, for example…

```
p.spaced-out {
  position: relative;
  top: 50px;
}
```

If you wanted a table pushed up and nudged left, you could write, for example…

```
table#adjusted {
  position: relative;
  bottom: 25%;
  right: 35%;
}
```

In relative positioning the other elements don't adjust to the relatively positioned element's altered position. They behave as if the element were in its normal position. So, as with absolute and fixed positioning, it's possible to have overlap. If necessary, you can solve this with a spacing tactic similar to the one you learned in Chapter 68.

In most circumstances, you don't have to tell the browser to position an element normally, since that's the default. But just so you know, a normally positioned element has *static* positioning.

```
div.normal {
  position: static;
}
```

In your CSS file, use relative positioning to move the **div** that you created for the last chapter to the right. Save the file. Display the page.

Sample CSS code is at
http://asmarterwaytolearn.com/htmlcss/practice-84-1.html.

Find the interactive coding exercises for this chapter at:
http://www.ASmarterWayToLearn.com/htmlcss/84.html

85
Z-INDEX

In the last chapter you learned that when you override the normal flow of a webpage by using fixed, absolute, or relative positioning, elements may overlap each other. Occasionally, you may want this to happen. For example, you might want to overlay a heading on top of an image.

You want the heading to be on top of the image, not the other way around. How do you tell the browser to put the heading on top? By specifying a **z-index** for the heading.

The higher the **z-index**, the higher it goes in the stack. An element with a **z-index** of 10 will sit on top of an element with a **z-index** of 9.

The default **z-index** of elements is 0. So if you give your heading a **z-index** of 1, it'll be placed on top of the image, which, assuming you haven't assigned it a **z-index**, has a **z-index** of 0.

```
h2#header {
   z-index: 1;
}
```

If you give it a **z-index** of -1, it'll be one layer below the default.

1. In your CSS file, code a **div** id.

2. Fix its position at the bottom-left.

3. Give it a **z-index** of -1.

4. In your HTML file, code the id. Place an image inside it: http://www.asmarterwaytolearn.com/monarch.jpg.

5. Save the files. Display the page. Scroll and see what happens.

Sample CSS code is at http://asmarterwaytolearn.com/htmlcss/practice-85-1.html. Sample HTML code is at http://asmarterwaytolearn.com/htmlcss/practice-85-2.html.

Find the interactive coding exercises for this chapter at:
http://www.ASmarterWayToLearn.com/htmlcss/85.html

86
MEDIA QUERIES

These days, you almost *have* to make your site *responsive*. That means creating custom styling for screens of different sizes, from the smallest phone to the largest desktop.

For example, five medium-size images arrayed across the screen are fine if the screen is 1280 pixels wide. But not if it's a 480-pixel iPhone screen. On a phone, you'll want to force them to stack vertically.

To create different style rules for different screens, you write *media queries*. For example, a media query asks, "Is the screen no wider than x pixels and no narrower than y pixels? If so, follow these style rules."

Responsive design can be a maddeningly complicated business and deserves a book of its own, but I want to give you a sense of how it works, so I'll show you one example.

There are various ways to incorporate media queries in your code. I'll show you how to add them to a stylesheet.

There are thirteen different media characteristics you can test for in a media query, including color and whether the user is looking at a mobile device in portrait or landscape orientation. I'll focus on the most common tests, for a screen of any kind (that is, not a printer) and for minimum device width and maximum device width.

Here's some code.

```
@media only screen and (min-device-width: 320px) and (max-
device-width: 480px) {
  img.gallery {
    display: block;
  }
}
```

The code above specifies **block**—that is, one on each line—for the "gallery" class of images when displayed on a phone, a device we define as having a minimum width of 320 pixels and a maximum width of 480 pixels.

Let's look at each piece of the code.

@media is how all media queries begin.

```
@media only screen and (min-device-width: 320px) and (max-
device-width: 480px) {
  img.gallery {
    display: block;
  }
}
```

only screen means the style rule applies only to devices with screens. This means it doesn't apply to printers.

```
@media only screen and (min-device-width: 320px) and (max-
device-width: 480px) {
  img.gallery {
    display: block;
  }
}
```

When you write **and** in a media query, you're saying, "The following must *also* be true in order for the style rule to apply." So it's not enough for the device to be a screen. It must be a screen **and** the minimum device width must be 320 pixels (portrait mode) **and** the maximum device width must be 480 pixels (landscape mode).

```
@media only screen and (min-device-width: 320px) and (max-
device-width: 480px) {
  img.gallery {
    display: block;
  }
}
```

The device-width specifications must be enclosed in parentheses.

```
@media only screen and (min-device-width: 320px) and (max-
device-width: 480px) {
  img.gallery {
    display: block;
  }
}
```

By writing **display: block**, you tell the browser not to float the images.

```
@media only screen and (min-device-width: 320px) and (max-
device-width: 480px) {
  img.gallery {
    display: block;
  }
}
```

The following media query tells the browser to float the images when they're displayed on a desktop or laptop, defined as having a minimum width of 1224 pixels. Note that there's no maximum width, since we're testing for just one orientation.

```
@media only screen and (min-device-width: 1224px) {
  img.gallery {
    float: left;
  }
}
```

1. In your CSS file, code a media query that styles a class of paragraph in the font-family "Comic Sans MS", cursive, sans-serif—if the screen is at least 800 pixels wide.

2. In your HTML file, code a paragraph of that class.

3. Save the files. Display the page.

Sample CSS code is at http://asmarterwaytolearn.com/htmlcss/practice-86-1.html. Sample HTML code is at http://asmarterwaytolearn.com/htmlcss/practice-86-2.html.

Find the interactive coding exercises for this chapter at:
http://www.ASmarterWayToLearn.com/htmlcss/86.html

87
MIN- AND MAX-WIDTH,
MIN- AND MAX-HEIGHT

Suppose you've styled a **div** to occupy 20% of the width of the screen. This works fine as long as the screen is large, but what happens on a phone with a 320-pixel screen? The **div** width shrinks to 64 pixels—a narrow stripe down the page with room for one or two words per line. To prevent this, you specify a **min-width**.

```
div#additional-info {
  width: 20%;
  min-width: 200px;
}
```

Now the **div** will run 20% of the width of the screen—but only as long as the width doesn't go below 200 pixels. When that point is reached, your CSS tells the browser to make the width 200 pixels.

Then there's the opposite problem. You've created a **div** that runs 40% of the width of the screen. A block of text inside this **div** might measure a user-friendly 12 to 14 words wide. But when the same page is displayed on an oversize screen, it could stretch to 20 words wide. That's too wide for easy reading. So you specify a **max-width**.

```
div#main {
  width: 40%;
  max-width: 500px;
}
```

Now, on a wide screen, the width will shrink to 500 pixels when 40% translates into more than 500 pixels.

You can also establish limits on height, using **max-height** and **min-height**.

```
p.article {
  min-height: 150px;
  max-height: 600px;
}
```

A problem occurs when the content of an element exceeds the **max-height** that you've specified for the element. In the example above, you tell the browser to limit the paragraph to a height of 600 pixels. If the text in the paragraph runs, say 750 pixels high, the text overflows, potentially creating a mess. You solve this with **overflow: hidden** or **overflow: scroll**.

In the following example, you tell the browser to make any overflowing content invisible.

```
p.article {
  min-height: 150px;
  max-height: 600px;
  overflow: hidden;
}
```

In the following example, you tell the browser to display a scroll bar that allows the user to scroll down to any overflow.

```
p.article {
  min-height: 150px;
  max-height: 600px;
  overflow: scroll;
}
```

1. In your CSS file, code a class of paragraph with a **max-width** of 100 pixels and a max-height of 100 pixels. Make the overflow scroll.

2. In your HTML file, code a paragraph of that class, including at least a dozen words.

3. Save the files. Display the page.

Sample CSS code is at http://asmarterwaytolearn.com/htmlcss/practice-87-1.html. Sample HTML code is at http://asmarterwaytolearn.com/htmlcss/practice-87-2.html.

Find the interactive coding exercises for this chapter at:
http://www.ASmarterWayToLearn.com/htmlcss/87.html

88
THE STUFF AT THE TOP

The standard code you find at the top of an HTML document is gobbledygook, but as a conscientious coder, you're always going to include it, so you may as well know what it means.

The first line in the document is the **doctype** declaration.

```
<!DOCTYPE HTML>
```

This tells the browser the document is written in HTML5. This is what you'll always write when you're creating a new document, whether the document has any HTML5 features in it or not. Things to notice:

1. The exclamation point.

2. It's in all-capital letters, a convention not a requirement.

3. There's no closing tag.

Next comes the **<html>** tag. To keep things simple, I've coded it minimally in previous chapters, but the recommended way to write it is like this.

```
<!DOCTYPE HTML>
<html lang="en">
```

That little bit of extra information tells the browser, the search engines, and screen readers that the text content of the page—the headings, paragraphs, and tables—are in English. If your page is in Italian, you'd write **lang="it"**; in Hindi, **lang="hi"**; etc. As you know, the **<html>** tag is closed with **</html>** at the end of the document.

The **<head>** tag, which you're familiar with, goes on the third line.

```
<!DOCTYPE HTML>
<html lang="en">
  <head>
```

It is closed with the **</head>** tag at the end of the head section. At a minimum, the head section contains…

```
<meta charset="utf-8">
```

This tag tells the browser to use a particular flavor of text encoding that permits the greatest variety of characters, thus accommodating the greatest number of languages. The tag isn't closed.

Next, you'll write opening and closing title tags. Inside them you'll write the text that will appear in the browser toolbar, in a bookmark list, and in search engine results. Give each page a unique title that describes its particular contents.

```
<!DOCTYPE HTML>
<html lang="en">
  <head>
    <meta charset="utf-8">
    <title>Characteristics of the Slow Loris</title>
```

In your HTML file, code the first two tags at the top of a document. Code the **meta charset** tag beneath the **head** tag. Save the file. Display the page to be sure your changes haven't broken anything.

Sample HTML code is at http://asmarterwaytolearn.com/htmlcss/practice-88-1.html.

Find the interactive coding exercises for this chapter at:
http://www.ASmarterWayToLearn.com/htmlcss/88.html

89
THE META DESCRIPTION

If you're hoping people will find your page through a search engine and then click on the link, you need a *meta description.* A good meta description doesn't improve your search ranking, but it does increase clicks, because search engines display the description in the search result. When I googled "Carlypso," Google displayed this result…

> www.**carlypso**.com
> Sell your car with **Carlypso**. Get up to 40%
> more than trade-in with the same convenience.

The two sentences following the link are the meta description coded into the Carlypso home page. Can you see why having Google display these sentences would increase the number of clicks?

You write the meta description in the head section of your page.

```
<head>
  <meta charset="utf-8">
  <title>Sell Your Car Hassle-Free</title>
  <meta name="description" content="Sell your car with
Carlypso. Get up to 40% more than trade-in with the same
convenience.">
```

Things to notice:

- It begins with **<meta name="description"**

- That's followed by **content=**

- Then comes the description itself, in quotes.

- There's no closing tag.

Some advice:

- Make your description as appealing as possible, but don't promise more than you can deliver.

- Search engines cut off a description after about 160 characters. That's a few more characters than a Twitter Tweet. Limit your description to that length.

- Don't repeat your title as a description.

- Give each page on your site a unique meta description.

Add a meta description to your HTML file. Save the file. Display the page to make sure your change hasn't broken anything.

Sample HTML code is at
http://asmarterwaytolearn.com/htmlcss/practice-89-1.html.

Find the interactive coding exercises for this chapter at:
http://www.ASmarterWayToLearn.com/htmlcss/89.html

90
BUILD A SITE

Look how far you've come, and how much HTML and CSS you've learned in a rather short time. Congratulations.

So now you're ready to build a site. (And if you're not totally ready, you know where to find the information you need if you forget how to do something: right here in this book.)

As a final project, I'm going to ask you to build a three-page site for your city, region, or country. It'll demonstrate the most important things you've learned in this book.

You don't have to do any original writing. All the content you need is at Wikipedia, your chamber of commerce, or any number of informational websites that cover your area.

You can create the site on your hard drive and run it off the drive, as you've been doing with the practice page. Or, if you have a website, you can upload it to your site. If you do publish the site, take care that you don't violate any copyrights when you copy content from other sites and paste it into your HTML files. (Wikipedia is safe.)

I've built an example site that you can use as a model. It's at http://www.asmarterwaytolearn.com/htmlcss/taos.html.

Find the CSS and HTML files for the site at:
http://www.asmarterwaytolearn.com/htmlcss/taos_css_code.html
http://www.asmarterwaytolearn.com/htmlcss/taos_code.html
http://www.asmarterwaytolearn.com/htmlcss/hiking_code.html
http://www.asmarterwaytolearn.com/htmlcss/skiing_code.html

I've heavily commented the first two files, to help guide you in building your own site.

For capturing images from the Web, I like the free utility from http://prntscr.com. (Again: don't violate anyone's copyright if you're going to publish.)

To crop and resize images online, the free http://picresize.com is excellent.

http://www.awardspace.com offers free hosting for a small website.

https://filezilla-project.org offers a free FTP client that makes it easy to upload your files to your web host.

Happy website building.

ACKNOWLEDGEMENTS

If you like the book and the online exercises, give a tip of the hat to these readers, who took the time to make corrections in the book and exercises. This program is now so much better because of their generosity.

James Foxworthy
John Koch
Jack McKinnon
Tim Miller
Jim Rohrer
Christopher Urrutia